VIOLENT CIVILITIES

ENGLISH, INDIA, CULTURE

TO J & THE MEMORY OF MY FATHER

VIOLENT CIVILITIES
ENGLISH, INDIA, CULTURE

Prem Poddar

 AARHUS UNIVERSITY PRESS

Violent Civilities
is printed by Narayana Press, Denmark
© Prem Poddar and Aarhus University Press 2002
Cover illustration: Anmole Prasad
Cover design: Lotte Bruun Rasmussen

ISBN 87 7288 767 2

Aarhus University Press
Langelandsgade 177
DK-Aarhus N
Phone (+45) 89 42 53 70
Fax (+45) 89 42 53 80

73 Lime Walk
Headington, Oxford OX3 7AD
Fax (01865) 75 00 79

P.O. Box 511
Oakville, Connecticut 06779
Fax (860) 945 9468

www.unipress.dk

Published with the financial support of
The Danish Research Council for the Humanities and
Aarhus University Research Foundation

Acknowledgments

The essays in this book were written in 1996 in Brighton, U.K. For various reasons I have been unable to deliver the essays to the press for the last five years. Were I to rewrite them in our post-9/11 world and in an India where the discourse of a knowledge economy seems to be in place, I would probably emphasise this and de-emphasise that in some of the arguments. But there would be no radical departures which would significantly alter my position.

Now that they are finally seeing the light of day, I take this opportunity to thank those people who were in one way or another involved in my thinking and writing of the book. First and foremost, my two critical readers and supervisors who shaped the work I was doing at the University of Sussex: Homi Bhabha and Brian Street.

Special thanks go to Rehnuma Ahmed, Imran Matin, David Johnson, Margareta Jolly, Graham MacPhee, Dawa Norbu, Erika Seki, Mahesh Daga, Durren, Elena Galtieri, Conor Macarthy, Heiko Henkel, Rangan Chakravarty, Vasu Jain, Prashanta Tripura, Tejaswini Apte, Marie-Jo Cortijo, Tanka Subba, Anmole Prasad, Anadi Chhetri, Harka Chhetri, Dorjee Lepcha, Khalid Nadvi, Frank Gloversmith, Jenny Taylor.

Finally, my thanks also go to the Foreign Office whose grant of a fellowship made the research possible in the first place, and to Birgitte Possing of Danmarks Humanistiske Forskningscenter for allowing me the space to collect my thoughts.

Contents

Introduction
'Supplemental Accounts'[1]

India a nation! What an apotheosis! Last comer to the drab nineteenth-century sisterhood! Waddling in at this hour of the world to take her seat ... Fielding mocked again.

Forster 1924/1980: 322

No Description of Great Britain can be what we call a finished Account, as no Cloaths can be the Likeness of a living Face; the Size of one, and the Countenance of the other always altering with Time ... .

Even while the Sheets are in the Press, new Beauties appear in several Places, and almost to every Part we are oblig'd to add Appendixes, and Supplemental Accounts of fine Houses, new Undertakings, Buildings, etc.

Defoe 1927 I: 4

What do we do with English studies in postcolonial India?[2] That was the question with which this project began, marking a phase of intense personal disquiet with the discipline of 'English literature'. The disquiet arose from an acute awareness of my own complicity in the discipline both as a student and a teacher. As a researcher, it became an opportunity, in a Gramscian phrase made famous by Said, to "inventory the traces upon me" and, in the process, to radically redefine the idea of English studies (Gramsci 1971: 324; Said 1979: 25).

Though motivated by personal history, I did not think of
my concerns as a lonely enterprise, an individual confrontation with one's subjectivity and place in the symbolic order,
but, in fact, as the imperative – even prerogative – of a
shared postcolonial predicament where history looms large
and the personal cannot but be located in the social and the
political.

Issues of pedagogy, curriculum, 'national' needs and educational reform are all central in defining the postcolonial
moment. Most of these issues, in turn, are framed in ways that
have significant continuities with the colonial discourse on
education. Thus, the question of English studies is both a fact
of India's colonial history and an ongoing problem for those
trying to think about and beyond that history.

The reason why political independence has not 'freed' the
discipline of English studies from its colonial moorings has
partly to do with the nature of colonialism's other: nationalism. The fact is that the discourse of nationalism, despite its
overt antipathy to alien rule, shared many of the same epistemic and axiological assumptions which motivated the colonial enterprise. In recent times, Partha Chatterjee, more than
any other theorist, has both questioned the thesis regarding
the fundamental 'derivativeness' of nationalist discourse and
underlined its complicity with the categories of Western
rationalism inherent in colonial discourse.

Despite some awareness of India as a fractured nation
brought together by the nationalist struggle, discursively
glued together by the ideals set forth in the founding text of
the Constitution, and continually reinforced by innumerable
official edicts, the 'Indian people' (here one does not really include the vast multitude of the voiceless) in general have – at
least until the 1970s – demonstrated little scepticism towards
the state's agenda and its promise of development for every
citizen. The nation-state as the primary interventionist force
for social reform, and standing for modernity, science, technology and secularism, was seen as heralding emancipation

from all kinds of evils. However, since the 1980s, the state's drive towards modernity has come under fire from various groups – women's movements, environmental activists, ethnic communities – who emphasise the failure of the state to protect and guarantee the distinctive and different identities of various minority groups.[3] The understanding of national culture as discourse allows us to see Indian national culture, to borrow Hall's phrase, as constituting a "discursive device" which represents difference as identity (1992: 297).

The concept of the nation as a discursive formation is, of course, central to my examination of how the Indian nation[4] has been articulated. In this book, I shall draw on the theorization of colonial discourse, attributed to imperial administrators and writers, by analysts like Said, Bhabha and Spivak, and in the later chapters, by way of critiquing the discourse of development, I shall consider the official discourse around English, education and culture.

The opening epigraph, taken from Daniel Defoe's *A Tour thro' the Whole Island of Great Britain*, envisions the nation as protean, as an organism that mutates over time. Defoe, here, addresses himself to what he sees as a national community in the process of becoming, and the simultaneous present of the modern that is shared by readers of serial publications generating a "community in anonymity" (Anderson 1983: 36). This notion of a constructed nation is apparent in the self-consciousness of not only Defoe's writing, but the writings of a host of other English writers. Their imagining of the British/English[5] nation ironically foreshadows the imagining of the Indian nation as an offshoot of colonial conquest. Attempting to counter the problems inherent in, for example, Said's dichotomous theorizing of Europe and the Orient, Dipesh Chakraborty has suggested the use of the term "hyperreal" to describe how both Europe and India are "figures of the imaginary". To treat them "as though they were given, reified categories, opposites paired in a structure of domination and subordination", he says, is to invite "the charge of

nativism, nationalism, or worse, the sin of sins, nostalgia"
(1992: 1). What are the consequences of such imaginings?

Recent thinking around cultural nationalism seems to come
up with one or other of three basic formulations. The modernist position (Anderson 1983; Gellner 1983) views nationalism as a hegemonic construction common to modern times. It
finds its genesis, particularly outside Europe, to be componen-
tially Western as well as indigenous, in opposition to colonial
rule as well as a mode of resistance/liberation from colonialism. This influential position appears in other guises. Norbu's
formulation, for instance, in his study of the culture and politics of Third World nationalism states: "the structure of
nationalism consists of two equally powerful components:
traditional data (such as race, language, literature, tradition,
territoriality) and egalitarian ideology (such as freedom,
equality and fraternity)" (1992: 1). With an alternative
terminology, Fishman's distinction between 'nationism' and
'nationalism' differentiates the role of politico-geographic
boundaries from ideological and socio-cultural identities in
nation formation. The 'new' nations, in contrast to the 'old',
began as political-geographical entities before their socio-
cultural identities emerged (1968).

The second position is the primordialist view, which appears
mostly in political and journalistic modes, in which suppressed
essentialist precolonial identities are seen resurfacing and re-
claiming ground lost to the occupying cultural order imposed
by foreign governance. In contradistinction to the 'Western'
civic-territorial model where the national states were produced by a "long process of ethnic bureaucratic incorporation", Smith sees the 'new' route of nation formation in terms
of the ethnic-genealogical model which was a consequence of
the mass mobilization of "'vernacularized' demotic *ethnie*
through a returning intelligentsia" (1994: 718).

The third, and newest, is the post-Orientalist, anti-essen-
tialist position (Dirks 1987; Chatterjee 1986; Inden 1990;
Pandey 1990) which argues that colonialism, through the

essentializing power of its discourse, reconfigured certain ethnic and cultural identities by imposing a certain 'order' arising
from the process, and then imposed those identities on those
it governed. The pre-existence of fluid identities, before this
epistemic violence wrought by colonization, thus leads to the
idea of the nation as fragmentary. In his critique of Western
rationality and its universalistic claims, Partha Chatterjee
emphasizes the fragmentary and subaltern perspective on the
nation. For any understanding of nationalist politics and the
"ideology of nationalism", a close scrutiny of nationalist
thought, "its claims about what is possible and what is
legitimate", and its status as a "discourse of power", becomes
essential (1986: 40-41). Nationalist thought in the colonial
world may be a different discourse (from Orientalism), but it
is dominated by and dependent on the post-Enlightenment
bourgeois-rationalist categories of knowledge. Employing a
framework supplied by the phenomenological categories of
'problematic' and 'thematic' (and also the Gramscian notion of
'passive revolution'), Chatterjee argues that the nationalist
'problematic' is the reverse of Orientalism; it embodies the
unquestioned premise inherent in the category of the Oriental, but grants "him" a subjectivity that is agentially active
and autonomous. Nationalism's 'thematic' or its justificatory
structures, however, are the same as Orientalism's: they depend on the distinction between East and West as an essential
and unchanging one (36-39). Nationalist thought thus becomes a contradictory mode of thought, its emancipatory
project standing compromised as it operates "within a framework of knowledge whose representational structure corresponds to the very structure of power [it] seeks to repudiate"
(38). The nation may be decolonized, but nationalism arrives
"at a false resolution which carries the marks of its own
fragility" (1986: 169).

   Nationalist affirmation, writes Said, must always be self-
reflexive and take account of the "incipient and unresolved
tension in the contest between a stable identity as it is

rendered by such affirmative agencies as nationality, education, tradition, language and religion on one hand, and all sorts
of marginal, alienated and anti-systemic forces on the other".
Said goes on to stress the role of intellectual negation and
skepticism in a climate of patriotism, of the assertion of cultural superiority and the development of mechanisms of control: "It is precisely in that nexus of committed participation
and intellectual commitment that we should situate ourselves
to ask *how much* identity, *how much* positive consolidation,
how much administered approbation we are willing to tolerate
in the name of our cause, our culture, our state" (1988: 46).

The uses of nation/nationalism in Third World literature
constitute the nation-building process, as well as realizations
of it: Bankim Chandra Chattopadhyaya's *Anandmath*, Balmukunda Gupta's *Shivashambhu Ke Chithe*, Raja Rao's *Kanthapura* ... . If one were to read Rushdie's *Midnight's Children* as an allegory,[6] then we would have to treat the novel as
a reflection on Indian history as text. The history that it takes
up is the official history of the nation, the history of the
nationalist bourgeois leadership. In various readings of the
novel, Rushdie is held up as the demystifier of nationalist
ideology (Brennan 1989) and as writing the 'excess' of the
nation-state (Bhabha 1989; Prakash 1990). I would like to
align myself to the view that "it explodes the notion of the
nation having a stable identity and a single history, then
invites a sceptical, provisional faith in the nation it has
exploded" (Kortenaar 1995: 41-42). That, in effect, albeit
without Rushdie's Nehru-like faith in the modern, sums up
my own position when I imagine India.[7]

This provisionality which counters provincialness, as in the
case of 'wandering peoples', can be seen as disrupting the borders of the modern nation. Older national signifiers become
displaced and spill over into "the imaginative geography of
metropolitan space" (Bhabha 1990b: 318). The narrative of a
historically linear nationhood, evidenced in the various governmental reports that I shall examine, becomes possible only

by the wilful repression of other narratives that could question its hegemony. The liminal time-space of the nation is represented by Bhabha as a 'double-time'. In this double-time, 'pedagogic' narratives (which claim to instruct us as to who we are) co-exist with 'performative' counter-narratives (Bhabha 1990b), which issue from the nation's margins and are articulated by cultural hybrids who live at the restless junction of several cultures. Such a hybridity invokes, and at the same time disturbs, the totalizing boundaries of the nation.

The nation-state is characterised by the fluidity of its boundaries and its proneness to fragmentation. United India, of course, is an internally riven and fractured entity: caste, class, ethnicity, language, etc., all generate their own fractures. Historians have pointed out that 'India' as such did not exist before colonization; what maps out as its nation-space today was just an amorphous collection of princely states with their own traditions and distinctive histories[8] (see Breckenridge and Van der Veer 1993). The modern Indian nation-state is rejected by analysts like Chatterjee (1986; 1994) and Spivak (1992) as a fabrication of the bourgeoisie which has minimal importance for the bulk of its subaltern population. To call it fabrication or invention, however, is not to say that some kind of India (e.g. *Bharatavarsha*) did not exist, whether mythically (as in the epic *Mahabharata*) or historically (as in the reign of Ashoka, c. 269-232 B.C.E.). Although the state of India formally came into existence in 1950 with its republic status, Kautilya's treatise on statecraft, *Arthasastra*, is indicative of a state tradition dating back to at least three centuries before Christ (see Thapar 1984).

This is not to be confused with the classicalization of tradition to which Orientalist scholars contributed, such that a cultural ancestry could be located in the Vedic age by nineteenth century nationalists attempting to forge the idea of a nation. In opposition to the 'materialist' West, they constructed an India of spiritual civilization. Swami Vivekananda and Rishi Aurobindo, for instance, spoke of the 'soul of India'. Thus,

Vivekananda writes: "Here in this blessed land, the foundation, the backbone, the life-centre is religion and religion
alone. In India, religious life forms the centre, the keynote of
the whole music of national life" (in Nirvendananda 1976: 6).
In this construction of a spiritualist India and a materialist
West, the emphasis on the co-existence of little traditions with
the Great Tradition,[9] as of the this-worldly *Panchatantra* and
Jataka tales with the metaphysical Upanishads, is completely
lost. And today, the perennialists' retrospective nationalism,
which involves reading features of modern nations into pre-
modern ethnic groups, can be seen in extreme programmes
like those of the right-wing Bharatiya Janata Party which
banks on the idea of an ancient and pure Hindu nation[10] (see
Basu et al 1993). In such versions, the idea of India as a culture
of plural space disappears (see Das 1989).

A state tradition entails the historical occurrence and communal recollections of the notion of stateness. Thus as a
response to the British presence, the nationalists requisitioned
images of the state as confiscator, as the guardian of law and
as enlightened partner. Nandy classifies images of the postcolonial state into three groups: as the keeper of tradition; as
the agency finally obligated for its formulation; and as a space
for the renegotiation of existing social arrangements (Nandy
1983).

The extent to which the Indian state fulfilled these roles or
can do so in the future is very much a function of the kind of
discourses it produces. Thus, when I look at the *Haksar Commission Report,* I stress its role as a legitimating device, the discourse it constitutes making possible the orchestration of
collective action by the state. This orchestration of action
directed towards the social formation at large is done in the
name of the interests of the people. The Commission's legal
and epistemological status invests it with authority, but its
investigation of facts is not disinterested as it occurs within
the elaboration of a particular idea of the state.

My concern in this book is chiefly the articulation of the

Indian nation in ruling discourses; both those of the colonizers and those of the nationalists who took over power in post-colonial India. I do not attempt to offer comprehensiveness of any kind; the book is more a suggestive work. I do not attempt to map the "marginal, alienated and anti-systemic forces" (Said 1988: 46), but point instead to the elisions that have been carried out in the name of a united nation.

What charge did English literature carry when it was brought to India? In what ways do official discourses on education and culture in postcolonial India define/articulate the nation in an attempt to distance themselves from the colonial configurations of English? And how can the continuing existence of English studies be justified in a centre/periphery dialectical relation? As colonial discourse theorists and critics like Said, Bhabha, Spivak, Hulme and other scholars have shown, representations of the colonized in literary and other texts (official documents, travel writings, diaries, etc.) served as an instrument of colonial expansion and helped reinforce already established colonial rule. Thus, my first chapter delineates the complex interventions of Bhabha and Spivak and their critical value in reading the postcolonial moment as it pertains to India. While I argue with them that a simple binary system between the developed and the developing is problematic, and that difference of all kinds has to be taken into consideration, I also question their (especially Bhabha's) seeming disregard for the mundanely material.

The second chapter is an overview of the discursive framework that led to the introduction of English education in the period of 'high imperialism', a period which begins around the middle of the nineteenth century (Morris 1979: 23). The colonial relationship that became forged between Britain and India during this period was marked by formal annexation and administration ritualised in the installation of Queen Victoria as the Empress of India in 1858 (see Hobsbawm 1987). I examine the statements of colonial administrators and particular writings on race and culture to foreground the interests that

impelled the introduction of English literature (and English
education in general). I then indicate how that was justified on
the grounds of the West's 'civilizing mission'. I do not wish to
de-emphasize the economic dimension of this project by
seeming to draw excessively from discourse theorists. As
Mitter succinctly phrases it, the challenge for the critic of
colonialism is precisely "how do we steer a precarious middle
course between economic determinism and a textual deconstruction that lacks an engagement with the real human issue
of exploitation?" (1995: 22). By no means do I attempt to provide an alternative to the "excesses of postcolonialism" (22),
but point to the fact that in looking at postcolonial India, it is
impossible to steer clear of economic and social factors.

The violence of colonialism on the represented who begin
to buy into their representation (see Fanon 1986) becomes
clear when we look at nationalist discourses which set out
self-consciously to counter such representations. Thus, one of
the main arguments running throughout the book is the
homonymy between colonialist and nationalist discourses.
The three phases of national consciousness that Fanon has
drawn out are thus essential to my account. I indicate, for instance, how figures like Keshab Chandra Sen or even Rammohun Roy occupied the first and/or second Fanonian phase
when the native intellectual responds with an assimilative
strategy, and then begins spewing up this assimilated
identity (Fanon 1967). In that schema, it was left to figures
like Gandhi to surpass the discursive structures imposed by
colonialism to emerge as what Nandy (1983) has called a
'non-player'.

There is therefore the imperative to unpack the premises of
the nationalist Nehruvian vision anchored in a development
discourse which confidently believed that the road ahead for
the newly independent states was the trajectory laid down by
the example of 'older' preceding states. My point is not the
simplistic one which contends that essentially the postcolonial
Indian nation-state was a capitalist formation dressed up in

socialist rhetoric. I argue, rather, that the very project of Enlightenment, whether in the form of a liberatory Marxist telos or some other capitalist utopia, is imbricated in a modernity that seems to allow little space for any other kind of cultural existence.

Thus, the official discourses on education, though ostensibly posed against the colonial heritage form, in fact, part of the same discursive space and are continuous with it. Piecemeal changes cannot bring about a transformation that goes beyond structures that have proved inadequate to the people they are meant to serve, and which have had violent consequences for them.

The third chapter analyses the discourses that have been constructed in order to define what culture is in the life of the nation. I look at the ambitious *Haksar Commission Report* that aims to contain the whole notion of an Indian national culture and claims to delineate the parameters within which a national identity operates. This is significant, in that the shadow of a colonial past seems to hover over it even whilst it attempts to forge in nationalist terms what it can express only in the language of Arnold, Mill, and other English writers.

The last chapter analyses English studies as a discipline in Indian universities and colleges. It also looks at the terms of the various committee reports that have justified the teaching of English literature and language. It discusses several critical accounts of Forster's *A Passage to India* as examples of disabling as well as enabling readings.

The concept of discourse is central to my understanding of the issues relating to English studies in postcolonial India. Thus, if my first chapter looks at the theorization of colonial discourse by analysts like Said, Bhabha, Spivak, and the second chapter at the colonial discourse generated by imperial administrators and writers, the following chapter (by way of critiquing the discourse of development) looks at the official discourse around culture. What do I mean when I use the term 'discourse'? There are many available definitions which vary considerably. I will not even begin to draw out its different usages in linguistics and linguistic theory but confine myself primarily to the notions that I find useful.

Thompson (1984) identifies discourse as drawn out sequences of discernibly occurring instances of utterances. These expressions suggest the relation between linguistic and non-linguistic activity. The elaboration of the idea of discourse that I particularly employ in this book is based on Foucault's theorization.

Developing the concept of discourse as the locus of an alternative theoretical model, Foucault, in *The Archaeology of Knowledge*, states that the object of discourse is not the referent, the thing referred to by a sign, but that it is discourse which constitutes objects. Discourses are "practices that systematically form the objects of which they speak. Of course discourses are composed of signs; but what they do is more than use these signs to designate things. It is this *more* that renders them irreducible to the language (*langue*) and to speech" (1972: 49). In simple terms, discourse is a cluster of statements that enable a way of speaking about and representing a certain kind of knowledge about a subject. When statements about a subject are produced within a particular discourse, the discourse allows the elaboration of the theme in a particular manner. The several statements that go to make up a discourse or a discursive formation "fit together because any one statement implies a relation to all others" (Hall 1992). The notion of discourse implies the unity of language and practice, thought and action; there is no splitting these domains. The production of knowledge through language is what constitutes discourse. Discourse itself is (produced by) practice. This practice is discursive in that it is engaged in the act of producing meaning. A discourse could be produced by various individuals in different institutional locales. Its cohesiveness or coherence does not rely on a unitary site, whether of subject or locale. Sites or positions are constructed by discourse, enabling the address and reception of speech. As Hall points out, "Anyone deploying a discourse must position themselves *as if* they were the subject of that discourse" (1992a: 292). This does not entail a closure as a discourse borrows from and lends itself to other discourses; it is thus subject to change.

In the shift from ideology to discourse, Foucault stresses the contextual dimension of discursivity in general:

The question posed by language analysis of some discursive fact or other is always: according to what rules has a particular statement been made, and consequently according to what rules could other similar statements be made? The description of the events of discourse poses a quite different question: how is it that one particular statement appeared rather than another? (1972: 27)

In other words, what is enunciated is a part of the grid that has its own history and conditions of existence. Foucault describes the procedures that control discourse as (i) prohibition or un-freedom to say just anything anytime anywhere; (ii) exclusion or rejection whereby 'abnormal' speech is silenced or treated differently; and (iii) erection of the opposition between true and false. Another set of procedures relate to structures of restriction. The "societies of discourse" limit the production and dissemination of discourse to certain doctrinal groups. "[I]n its distribution, in what it allows and what it prevents", an education system, for instance, allows the social appropria-tion of discourse but the lines are "marked out by social distances, oppositions and struggles. Any educational system is a political way of maintaining or modifying the appropria-tion of discourses, along with the knowledges and powers which they carry" (1981: 64).

The 'will to knowledge' creates arrangements for the study of objects. The educational system, learned societies, libraries, the values set by different social systems on different forms of knowledge, comprise the institutional base on which the will to truth operates. Each society has its own 'regime of truth', its types of discourse regarded as true. The important questions then relate to how discourses are produced and how they produce 'normalized' individuals. The regime of truth that tells us what is true in India is largely composed of discourses that can broadly be classed as official and developmental.

These governmental and developmental discourses constitute the notion of 'discipline' that ambiguously serves both sides of the power-knowledge equation in Foucault: a procedure of correction and control as well as a branch of knowledge. In the context of colonial India, as I discuss in the second chapter of the book, the procedures of control are partly constructed through the discipline of English studies as is the constitution of a particular discipline, both narrowly and widely, India and English literature. The discursive effects of creating subjects in a form of self-government (submitting to an idealized self) is at the very heart of a disciplinary mechanism, which in turn is part of larger cultural apparatuses. Such power relations allow a subject to come into being but not without the capacity to resist. Witness this remark from a student in a college in India: "When the last Englishman with the thoughts of empire has perished, Enid Blyton will still be around converting a few more colonials, who will forever dream of potted meat sandwiches and buttered scones at four p.m. on Sundays, to the Christian universe" (quoted in Rajan 1992: 82). The danger, of course, is of a simple substitution of terms such that a nationalist agenda keen to revert to a certain tradition, or even a modernist programme that seeks to reimagine the nation, rules out the claims of a productive hybridity.

Notes

1 The nation as excess, as always in medias res and demanding a 'supplement' is captured in the passage I quote from Defoe. Derrida's account of 'supplement' stresses that all representation requires a

supplementary element in that it can never just feed upon that which is to be represented. "The sign is always the supplement of the thing itself" (1976: 144-45).

2 The term 'postcolonial' will be taken up later to indicate what its different usages are and what it has come to signify for various literary and cultural theorists and critics. Loosely speaking I am using it to signify a post-independent India, but not interchangeably: I need to emphasize the 'post' not as some kind of historical time/event marker but as a space that is contiguous with the colonial. In that sense there are parallels with the different meanings attributed to the notion of the 'postmodern'. Whenever I use a hyphen in the 'postcolonial', it is to denote that it is a period term, referring to a time after the Second World War, or the era after decolonisation. In 'Notes on the Post-Colonial', Ella Shohat stresses the need for an interrogation of the term as it leads "to a blurring of perspectives" (1992: 110). She calls for a historical, geographical, and cultural contextualization of the concept. "My argument is not necessarily that one conceptual frame is 'wrong' and the other is 'right', but that each frame illumines only partial aspects of systemic modes of domination, of overlapping collective identities, and of contemporary global relations" (111-12). Ironically, Spivak, who is considered to be one of the seminal postcolonial theorists, has dismissed the term completely: "I find the word postcolonialism totally bogus" (in Young 1991: 224). Anne McClintock questions the orientation of postcolonial theory which "in its premature celebration of the pastness of colonialism, runs the risk of obscuring the continuities and discontinuities of colonial and imperial power" (1994: 294). (See also Dirlik 1994 and Hall 1996.)

3 The post-70s were marked by the breakdown of many consensuses. Resurgence of fundamentalisms, increase of communal conflicts, caste wars, rise of secessionist movements, etc., were events which indicated that different groups were striving to articulate their identities in a manner which suggested to some (for instance, Upadhyay 1992) a state of civil war threatening the united nation. Vandana Shiva's book *Staying Alive: Women, Ecology and Survival in*

India (1988), for instance, is a record of grassroot resistance against capitalist and western ideas of development. These struggles, she argues, are informed by alternative notions of community, nature and development.

4 I am drawing here from Stuart Hall's notion of 'articulation'. He plays on the double sense of the term to suggest both utterance, expression and knitting together. Hall argues that cultural practices and texts are not etched with a final meaning by the intentions of production. Meaning arises out of an act of articulation within particular social relations (Hall 1981). The nation can thus be seen as/in the active process of production.

5 The British nation is mainly a re-fashioning of the English nation despite the Welsh, Scottish and Irish elements in its make-up. Gargi Bhattacharya makes much the same point: "English culture remains the dominant term within the idea of the British nation" (1991: 19). See also Dodd (186).

6 I am not entering here into the debate sparked off by Frederic Jameson's essay which argues that all "Third World cultural productions" are amenable to be read as national allegories because *"the story of the private individual destiny is always an allegory of the embattled situation of the public third world culture and society"* (1986: 69; emphasis in original). Aijaz Ahmad takes up Jameson and points to the impossibility of positing a global theory of third world literature. Ahmad asserts that we inhabit one world and the notion of a "third world" is not empirically based (1987: 7-9; this essay is reproduced in Ahmad 1992).

7 Rushdie clearly sides with the secular modernist Nehru's imagining of India as opposed to Gandhi's. While reviewing Attenborough's film *Gandhi*, Rushdie betrays his preference in the choice that India had between "Nehru, the urban sophisticate who wanted to industrialize India, to bring it into the modern age, [and] the rural, handicraft-loving, sometimes medieval figure of Gandhi" (1991: 104).

8 Sumit Sarkar makes the charge against the Congress party that "The Congress fought against the Raj, but it was also progressively becoming the Raj ... merely substituting the brown for the white" (1983: 4).

9 Robert Redfield, in his *Peasant Society and Culture,* refers to the
   interactions between "a great tradition of the reflective few" and "a
   little tradition of the largely unreflective many" (1956: 41).

10 With the rise of Hindu fundamentalism what is threatened, according to scholars like Ashis Nandy, is the traditional form of Hinduism which regards religion as essential to tolerance and co-survival.

CHAPTER ONE

'News From the Power-Lines'
Transporting Postcolonial Theory

This chapter will look at some recent trends in (post)colonial discourse theory and determine the degree of their translatability into the present Indian milieu. Drawing upon, in the main, the writings of Gayatri C. Spivak and Homi K. Bhabha, it will explore the problems inherent in the existence of English studies in India. A more exhaustive account of postcolonial discourse theory is not intended here, as that will necessarily assume that the moment and reach of such a theory is well defined and operates either within a single paradigm or multiple ones that are easily cohering/juxtaposable. Neither of the assumptions is tenable; the theorizing of postcolonial discourse is demonstrably multivocal. This implies that only those issues which possess some immediacy in relation to my project will be raised. I will engage with latent questions about neocolonialism and nationalism in the later sections and shall only refer to them here when required.

The idea is not to suggest that the disciplinary contours of English studies at the periphery are a function of master categories generated by these (and other) theorists located at the centre. Instead, the objective is to interrogate some of the assumptions and strategies of these critics in the light of existing or potential transgressive impulses emanating from 'real' formations at the periphery. In fact, this simple model of centre-periphery relations is already complicated by the fact that both theoreticians hail from India while being professionally located in the centres that engage in and produce theory.

CENTRE-PERIPHERY THEORY FLOWS

Since the Second World War (to indulge in familiar Eurocentrism) various terms have been invented to provide co-ordinates for the global condition. Thus, we have classificatory schemas like 'First/Second/Third World', 'developed/developing/undeveloped', 'centre/periphery' and 'North/South'. Economic and social indicators fashioned in the West have been deployed to categorise the different worlds and their levels of 'development'. "Yet," as Anthony King points out, "if this classification were reinterpreted to refer historically to those societies which, racially, ethnically, socially and culturally first approximated to what today are the culturally diverse, economically, socially and spatially polarised cities in the West but also, increasingly major cities round the world, what is now the Third World would historically more accurately be labelled the First World, and the First World would become the Third" (1993: 8). The discursive constructs, though ideologically motivated, are deployed as though they have an axiomatic ontological status. (Wolff 1993: 166-67).

The global dimension of cultural production and dissemination is now conventional knowledge; and so also is the conception of the world as an interconnected place or system. Thus Immanuel Wallerstein:

the only kind of social system is a world-system which we define quite simply as a unit with a single division of labour and multiple cultural systems. It follows logically that there can, however, be two varieties of such world systems, one with a common political system and one without. We designate these respectively as world empires and world economies. (1974: 390)

Similarly, Appadurai's (1990) model of the culture of capitalist international economy, in which he formulates a 'chaos-
theoretic' approach to 'non-isomorphic' flows, offers critical
resources for reading the postcolonial condition. Firstly there
are

ethnoscapes produced by flows of people: tourists, immigrants, refugees,
exiles and guest workers. Secondly, there are *technoscapes*, the machinery and plant flows produced by multinational and national corpora-
tions and government agencies. Thirdly, there are *financescapes*, produced by the rapid flows of money in the currency markets and stock
exchanges. Fourthly, there are *mediascapes*, the repertoire of images of
information, the flows which are produced and distributed by news-
papers, magazines, television and film. Fifthly, there are *ideoscapes*,
linked to flows of images which are associated with state or counter-
state movement ideologies which are comprised of elements of freedom,
welfare, rights, etc. (as paraphrased in Featherstone 1990: 6-7)

However, what is surprisingly missing from these formulations is the aspect of resistance to globalisation. As Stuart
Hall has reminded us, it would be erroneous to think of globalization as a non-contradictory, uncontested space. With the
margins increasingly achieving representation "marginality
has become a powerful space" (1993: 34). In a similar vein,
Abu Janet Lughod (1993) has argued for looking at processes
from the bottom up, that is, from the periphery to the centre,
which means speaking of "de-localization" instead of globalization.

What is the nature of transnational transfer in terms of
literature and literary theory? W.J.T. Mitchell, writing in the
Chronicle of Higher Education, sets up an interaction between
theorizing of the poststructuralist kind in the first world and
literary practices in the postcolonial world, which seems
almost like a 'fair' exchange – or as he terms it, a healthy "collaboration":

The most important new literature is emerging from the colonies –
regions and peoples that have been economically and militarily dominated in the past – while the most provocative new literary criticism is
emanating from the imperial centres that once dominated.

Even the most ordinary academic critic can now aspire to participate
in a global network of … 'Travelling theory', in which critics fly between conferences on semiotics, narratology, and paradigm changes in
places like Hong Kong, Canberra, and Tel Aviv. (1989: B1)

Mitchell speaks of an "intelligent, peaceful, and productive
decolonisation" of the third world as a *fait accompli*, making a
celebratory virtue of what is in effect a historical necessity. In
eliding differences of class, race, and most importantly, power
between nations, his position, in its political implications, is
aligned with a 'born-again' breed of 'neo-imperialist' ob-
servers who advocate that 'failed' or 'unreformable' (postcolonial) nation-states – which were once granted freedom but
made a mess of self-rule – must be returned to some kind of
Euro-American 'trusteeship'.[1]

Ironically, though, Mitchell's point is not entirely a novel
one. As will become clearer in my account of the introduction
of English literature in the nineteenth century and the continuities that such a legacy finds in the postcolonial existence of
the discipline, literary critics, especially in English departments of universities located in the British ex-colonies, have
always relied in their trade on the prevailing critical practices
in Anglo-American academia (although influence from the
U.S. is of relatively recent origin).

In 1905, when A.C. Bradley commented on the effects of
Shakespearean tragedy, he emphasized the feeling of rever-
ence that it generated for the dominant order based on a righteous principle: "the spectacle does not leave us rebellious or
desperate" (36). Bradley's remarks, developed from an Aris-
totelian notion of catharsis, were duly echoed by John Clark,
the Arderne Professor of English at Cape Town University
from 1903 to 1928, a few years later when he wrote: "the

spectacle does not leave us hopeless in our thoughts or insurgent in our attitude"[2] (1912: 30). In their Indian edition of
Othello published from Bangalore in 1928, Ram Gopal and P.
R. Srigamachari enthusiastically endorse Bradley's definition
of tragedy. "Prof. Bradley's brilliant exposition" is requisitioned to drive home Shakespeare's 'universality': "[I]n view
of Shakespeare's catholicity of sentiments, and his recognition
of human kinship, he belongs to the world"(xvi). As if not
convinced by their own argument about the Bard's transcul-
tural appeal, they go on to quote with approval the view of the
Ceylonese art critic Dr A. Coomarswamy, who insists: "In
times past, it has, indeed been fashionable to insist upon a supposed fundamental divergence of Europe and Asiatic character
[...] But the premises were false: the divergences of character
are false. For, the deeper we penetrate, the more we discover an
identity in the inner life of Europe and Asia" (1928: lxxxv).[3]

Enunciation, as we now know, is always positioned in
discourse. But when discourse claims that it is unpositioned –
in other words when it tries to speak for everybody – "it mis-
takes itself as a universal language", ignoring the fact that it
comes "out of a specific history ... a specific set of power
relations ... within a tradition" (Hall 1993: 36). As I will show
later, it is still fashionable to treat discourse as universal or not
belonging to *a* particular tradition, even though Leavisite
criticism now reigns supreme in the Indian academy.

Indian editions of Shakespeare still glorify Bradley; a
teacher in my own university in India spoke of Bradley as the
ultimate authority on the dramatist.[4] While Leavisite criticism awaits its dislodgement, 'theory' is slowly making its
way into some of the universities. (Articles with titles like
'Figural Isotopes in Paul de Man's Literary Theory'[5] and 'A
Deconstructionist Reading of *Moonstone*'[6] have recently begun to appear in Indian journals.) But the general antipathy
to Theory is exemplified by C.D. Narasimhaiah, one of the
most well-known critics of English, American, and Commonwealth literature in India, who dismisses the new critics – the

structuralists, post-structuralists and deconstructionists – as "rewriting the texts without having to read them" (quoted in Ramachandra 1991a: 1-2) and shows his impatience with "our thoughtless leaning towards structuralist and post-structuralist theories, ignoring *our own critical heritage*" (quoted in Ramachandra 1991b: 73; emphasis supplied). For critics like Narasimhaiah, the nationalising of Leavis, Bradley, etc. is what constitutes the 'critical heritage'. The question as to why post-structuralism – and not Leavisite criticism – is immediately identified as imperialist is not raised. Given the present theoretical directions, the term 'Derridean' could well be replacing 'English' in the metropolis, or so we are told by Radhakrishnan (1987: 212-13), but the move towards 'theory' in India cannot be condemned as long as its deployment raises wider questions relating to context, although there is no easy transference of terms.[7]

Although 'Commonwealth Literature' and Indian Literature in English have been consecrated in the Indian academy for over two decades, there has been little change in the terms of criticism. The old critical vocabularies, inherited from Mathew Arnold and F.R. Leavis, are still dominant. The expansion of the canon is calculated more to accommodate the urgencies of academic specialisms and less to reflect a 'theoretical' engagement with colonialism, race, gender and language.

The intrusion – and now rise – of colonial discourse theory in the Anglo-American academy poses a challenge to the existing configurations of literary studies. In many universities the challenge has been partially contained by inserting marginalised texts dealing with colonialism into reading lists of some courses, or by foregrounding more politicised readings of already canonized texts such as *The Tempest*, *Heart of Darkness*, and *Kim*. But the challenge comes straight to the centre in questioning the very notion of literariness. The text's relation to the world, as the critics have forcefully demonstrated in their readings, continues to implicitly point to the nexus between colony and empire. Thus, Said, for instance, shows how Jane Austen's *Mansfield Park* continues to link colonialism with domestic morality "right up to the last sentence" (1993: 111).

Furthering his critical account of the construction of the Orient as an object of disciplinary knowledge in *Orientalism* (1979), Said argues for the necessity of delineating the 'worldliness' of the text in a collection of essays entitled *The World, the Text, and the Critic*. Worldliness for him is a strategic positioning of the critic engaged in a kind of "affiliation study". Drawing upon Gramsci's notion of cultural ensembles and the function of hegemony in guiding intellectual activity, Said maintains that "[t]o recreate the affiliative network" is to

make visible, to give materiality back to, the strands holding the text to society, author, and culture ... . Affiliation releases a text from its isolation and imposes upon the scholar or critic the presentational problem of historically recreating or reconstructing the possibilities from which the text arose. Here is the place for intentional analysis and for the effort to place a text in homological, dialogical, or antithetical relationships with other texts, classes, and institutions. (1985: 174-75)

Said relies on poststructuralist theory for many of his formulations but stops short of advocating a decentred subject, retaining a role for subjectivity or human agency in the constitution as well as the disruption of discourse. Without the possibility of subjective autonomy, any political project would be unthinkable for Said.

In its unpacking of power-knowledge formations, poststructuralism may have provided the necessary inspiration and tools of analyses which enable the cultural critic to read the postcolonial moment. However, any uncritical or blanket extension of this approach to contexts other than the capitalist first world, where it originated, runs the risk of replicating the same neocolonial relations which it has otherwise done much to counter. Some colonial discourse critics would, of course, argue that the tradition of anti-imperialist critique goes back several decades before poststructuralism even entered the literary critical scene. The old writings of Lenin and V. G. Kiernan, not to mention the early work of the Frankfurt school, which in many ways anticipated the poststructuralist critique of subject-centred rationality at the heart of Enlightenment, can be cited in evidence. Equally, contemporary theorists such as Habermas and others have carried, albeit within the broad rubric of a modernist project, the Frankfurt tradition forward, thus providing a major theoretical alternative to poststructuralist theory.

What then is the vitally crucial purchase that poststructuralism promises and/or brings forth? The question, I hope, will be answered while taking account of the two theorists I now move on to discuss. The presupposition in my explication so far of a neat binarism between the first and the third world – albeit without any intention of essentializing or totalizing them – is no doubt simplistic and it is precisely for this reason that Spivak and Bhabha self-consciously negotiate their own location and imbrication in the versions of French theory they deploy.

Spivak: 'Strategic Essentializing'

Spivak's readings of cultural artefacts from the periphery are specially invested with authority in the third world because she is of the third world, even as she brings (and is) the latest news from the centre(s) of intellectual ferment. Conversely, her authority in the first world is in part to do with the fact that she makes her Indian passport visible while speaking of regions with which she has had first hand acquaintance. "[O]ne of the major arguments" running through the corpus of Spivak's writings, writes Colin MacCabe in the 'Foreword' to *In Other Worlds: Essays in Cultural Politics,*

is that the academy is constituted so as to be unable to address the most serious of global questions, and that, many of the most radical critiques remain completely within terms set out by the constituted academy. Spivak's theme here is large: the micro-politics of the academy and its relation to the macro-narrative of imperialism. (1987: x)

Her reading of the Indian fiction writer Maheswata Devi's 'Draupadi' is a case in point (1987). Spivak rereads the short story so as to politicise it in the context of the academy. The macro-politics of imperialism (in this case the role of the Indian state as an instrument of internal colonialism) is collapsed allegorically into the microphysics of power in academic relations.

In Spivak's hands, Senanayak, a character who represents state power and terrorism, becomes "the closest approximation to the first world scholar in search of the third world" (180); Spivak attributes responsibility to the author Maheswata Devi for the presentation of Senanayak as a "pluralist aesthete" (179). (Pluralist aesthetes of the first world cannot but be "willy nilly, participants in the production of an exploitative society" (179).) This characteristic enables him to identify, in theory, with his "object of study" his enemies; but at the same time it also allows him to participate "in the production of an exploitative society" on account of "necessities and contingencies" of his historical moment. This split in self accounts for the ambiguity of his emotions when his enemy Dopdi, a 'tribal' peasant woman waging a guerilla war against the landlords and their protectors, is brought before him as captive.[8] The ambivalent feelings of "[s]orrow (theory) and joy (practice)" that he experiences are linked to what the first world scholar is supposed to go through:

… we grieve and rejoice that they must lose themselves and become as much like us as possible in order to be 'free'; we congratulate ourselves on our specialists' knowledge of them. Indeed, like ours, Senanayak's project is interpretive: he looks to decipher Draupadi's song … . His self-image for that uncertain future is Prospero. (179)

This projection of Senanayak as an emblem of the first world scholar for whom the third world is a profession and an area of study[9] also entraps Spivak as critic. She is quick to acknowledge the imbrication but makes the case for an extenuating and somewhat redeeming difference in her location:

> Situated within the current academic theatre of cultural imperialism, with a certain *carte d'entree* into the elite theoretical ateliers of France, I bring news of power-lines within the palace. (221)

What lessons are there for the first world intellectual in the story that enacts "the undoing of the binary opposition between the intellectual and rural struggles" and breaks "the apparently clean gap between theory and practice in Senanayak"? (182). Spivak's recommendation is couched in these terms:

> If our certitude of the efficient-information-retrieval and talk to the accessible approach toward third world women can be broken by the wedge of an unreasonable uncertainty, into a feeling that what we deem gain might spell loss and that our practice should be forged accordingly, then we would share the textual effect of 'Draupadi' with Senanayak. (185)

Her article 'French Feminism in an International Frame' (1987) raises similar issues in terms of what the first world feminist scholar can offer to women in the third world who are objects of their investigation. A nineteenth century literary history without adequate reference to imperialism or certain modes of cultural representation that masquerade as 'empirical' history can only be constructed from the viewpoint and mindset of the discovering power. Spivak finds anti-humanist as well as radical historians guilty, even if inadvertently, of remaining entrenched in the structures they otherwise try so hard to dismantle. The assumption, for instance, behind the constitution of the category 'third world woman' by western feminist discourse is that there is no heterogeneity, that it is a group accessible to universal modes of analyses common to some versions of social anthropology. Anthropology, of course, has deconstructed this (see Mohanty 1988). The irony, however, is that in this current form of colonial discourse, the first world feminist manufactures a self-consolidating other as it (i.e. the third world woman) figures in history and literature (153).

In her reading of another Maheswata Devi story, 'Stana-dayani' or 'Breast-Giver', Spivak unpacks the assumptions of western criticism built into certain feminist positions (1987). The protagonist Joshoda is the breast-giver to the children of the upper class women, the *bhadramahilas*, who are thus freed from the task of breast-feeding. This is in direct opposition to the ideal of feminism in the first world as far as motherhood and individual female subjectivity are concerned. Jashoda, in other words, has no subjectivity. It is her body, particularly in the metonymic function of the cancer in her breast, that takes on the silent speech of decolonization and the failure of foster-mothering. In Joshoda, Spivak builds up a figure who can "articulate truths which speak of our as well as their situation" (1987: xvi).

Her readings are operations whose intention is the disclosure, in her words, of "ideology in action". The strategies she employs in her practice of reading are offered in four propositions:

a. The performance of these tasks, of the historian and the teacher of literature, must critically "interrupt each other, bring each other to crisis, in order to serve their constituencies; especially when each seems to claim all for its own.

b. The teacher of literature, because of her institutional subject-position, can and must "re-constellate" the text to draw out its use. She can and must wrench it out of its proper context and put it within alien arguments.

c. If thus placed in the arguments from Western Marxist Feminism,

Western Liberal Feminism, and French high theory of the Female
Body, "Stanadayani" can show us some of their limits and limitations.

d. This might have implications for the current and continued subalternization of so-called "third world" literatures. (1987: 241)

There is here a specific intellectual locale – that of critical theory in the English speaking first world – that Spivak seems to
be concerned about, as set out in the third proposition above.
Her second proposition of "re-constellat[ing]" Maheswata
Devi's text, 'Stanadayani', so as to help interrogate high theory comes bound with a heavy charge: the critic has to "wrench
it out of its proper context and put it within alien arguments".
The positive result of such a strategy rests well with her
declared goal of making visible "the current and continued
subalternization of so-called third world literatures". The con-
comitant fallout, however, is sometimes the all-too-easy recuperation of the "proper context": Spivak's own reading of
'Draupadi' forsakes any direct engagement with the historical
significance of the Naxalbari uprising which provides the
frame for the story. Her undervaluing of this moment is all
the more significant in that she addresses her arguments to a
metropolitan audience for whom this peasant rebellion is of
no direct concern and has no resonances. What of a critical
strategy, a pedagogy, that seeks "to at least entertain" (241)
these propositions in a nation-space in the third world? In her
essay 'Poststructuralism, Marginality, Post-coloniality and
Value', Spivak states that the "persistent critique of what one
must inhabit [...] involve[s] an incessant re-coding of diversified fields of value" (1990a: 226).

   This form of critique best serves its purpose when it brings
to crisis the attempts of revisionary modes of thinking to
negotiate and/or limit the effects of epistemic force. "If academic and 'revolutionary' practices do not bring each other to
productive crisis, the power of the word has clearly passed
elsewhere" (1990: 219). Her own practice involves the decon-

struction of the discourse of colonialism so as to bring to the fore the scaffolding of contradictory ideas concealed within its purported rationality. This allows her to draw out the contradictions that delimit the postcolonial condition.[10] Postcoloniality, thus, is a moment, a modernity (or contra-modernity if you will), that is subject to the defining categories forged during the experience of colonialism. "[W]hatever the identitarian ethnicist claims of native or fundamental origin", she writes:

> the political claims that are most urgent in decolonized space are tacitly recognized as coded within the legacy of imperialism: nationhood, constitutionality, citizenship, democracy, even culturism. Within the historical frame of exploration, colonization, decolonization – what is being effectively reclaimed is a series of regulative political concepts, the supposedly authoritative narrative of whose production was written elsewhere, in the social formations of Western Europe. They're being reclaimed, indeed claimed, as concept-metaphors for which no historically adequate referent may be advanced from postcolonial space, yet that does not make the claims less important. (225)

This condition of postcoloniality confers citizenship as opposed to subjecthood during coloniality. But the lineage in both cases is to be traced from the Enlightenment which becomes the locus of the critic's combative arena, the agenda of an anti-Eurocentric praxis. The will to disidentify with Europe is caught up in a paradox in Indianist discourse stretching from the inception of the nationalist struggle till the present efforts of decolonizing culturalists. The paradox is to catch up with modernity as it is bounded within the covenant of post-Enlightenment European ideas and ideals.

Postcolonial identity, as a result, is the product of history; it derives from configurations of a discursive aftermath. It is, according to Spivak, a concept-metaphor and not an ontology. Since concept-metaphors derive their significance discursively, they can be seen as manifestations of catachresis:[11] "[A] concept-metaphor without an adequate referent is a catachresis. These claims for founding catachreses make postcoloniality a deconstructive case" (225). The postcolonial condition becomes possible and is circumscribed by a non-existent referent. The absence of this ontological referent nevertheless leaves open the discursive space created by the Enlightenment in the ideals embodied in its texts; the postcolonial desire to attain modernity is thus a leap of faith.

This enables Spivak to locate, and to name agency. Postcoloniality can now be put forward as strategy:

> Postcoloniality as agency can make visible that the basis of all serious ontological commitment is catachrestical, because negotiable through the information that identity is, in the larger sense, a text. It can show that the alternative to Europe's long story – generally translated as 'great narratives' is not only short tales (petit recits) but tampering with the authority of storylines. (229)

As this passage makes evident, Lyotard's privileging of local narratives over the grand ones, which are now seen as having outlived their time, is not Spivak's agenda. The alternative to the metanarratives, for her, is disruption, "the tampering with the authority of storylines". The rejection of Marxism by Lyotard on the grounds that it is a grand narrative is thus not acceptable to Spivak. Even though she disclaims it, the idea of deconstruction as ideology-critique and her debt to Althusser is quite clear. For instance, in her essay 'The Ideology of Interpretation', she avers: "Ideology in action is what a group takes to be natural and self-evident, that of which the group, as a group, must deny any historical sedimentation. It is both the condition and the effect of the constitution of the subject (of ideology) as freely willing and consciously choosing in a world that is seen as background" (1987: 118).[12] Her complex attitude towards ideology-critique arises again in her essay 'Can the Subaltern Speak: Speculations on Widow Sacrifice':

In the face of the possibility that the intellectual is complicit in the persistent constitution of the Other as the Self's shadow, a possibility of political practice for the intellectual would be to put the economic "under
erasure," to see the economic factor as irreducible as it reinscribes the
social text, even as it is erased, however imperfectly, when it claims to
be the final determinant or the transcendental signified. (1988: 280)

Her reluctance to let go of the economic dimension as it operates in and within the "social text", and at the same time to
deny the determinism built into the formulations of Althusser, complicates her position. Textuality in the "larger sense"
embraces the socio-economic scope of political and cultural
formations. Colonialism is thus only a part of imperialism
which manifests itself in different forms in the neo-colonial
setting. Although critiquing her "transcendentalizing ges-
ture" toward Marxism, Robert Young makes much the same
suggestion: "Spivak moves the question of history into the
historical present of its writing: overall she is concerned less
with the process of historical retrieval or reinterpretation of
colonialism as such than with a critique of the forms of neocolonialism in the contemporary academy – hence her focus
on imperialism rather than the narrower historical form of
colonialism" (1990: 158).[13]

The continuity and the materiality of colonialism in the
world economic order as we inhabit it, the participation (however oppositional) of the intellectual in it, leaves no option for
Spivak other than to treat the world as text. But, unlike Said,
she foregrounds political economy to the extent that the cultural text has to be placed alongside (if not negotiated with)
Marx's exposition of the role of value in the "self-determin-
ation of capital".

In drawing from Marx, Spivak focuses, especially in her essays, 'Scattered Speculations on the Question of Value' (1987)
and 'Speculations on Reading Marx: After Reading Derrida'
(1987a), on his analysis of the commodity. Cultural politics
must grapple with the notion of value as it appears in use-

value. The discursivist bias of current cultural studies, she
feels, has too hastily done away with economics in an attempt
to escape any hint of economic determinism. The reason for
trying to bring it back in, Rey Chow maintains, is that "the
'economic' occupies a place in Spivak's reading that is similar
to 'center' in Jacques Derrida" (1993: 3). Marx's contention
that value resides and points to labour is qualified by Spivak
in order to argue that value is not just labour's "representation", which leads to "culturalism", but that it is irreducibly
material (1987: 168). If value is thus not the representation of
labour, it can be usefully seen as difference in the Derridean
sense of writing as *differance*. She says:

[T]he basic premise of the recent critique of the labour theory of value
is predicated on the assumption that, according to Marx, Value represents labour.

    Yet the definition of Value in Marx establishes itself not only as a
representation but also as a differential. What is represented or represents itself in the commodity-differential is Value. (158)

Her reworking of the theory of value introduces an element of
indeterminacy. The teleological unfolding in which labour
(read value) moves on to money which in turn is transformed
into capital in the standard Marxian account is not acceptable
to her.[14] The value of the commodity inheres not simply in the
use-value and certainly not in the exchange-value which
capitalist trade-relations tend to naturalize. The differential
between use-value and exchange-value is what Marx, according to her reading, is writing about:

... Marx is writing, then, of a differential representing itself or being
represented by an agency ... no more flexible than the empty and ad hoc
place of the investigator or community of investigators (in the field of
economics, planning, business management). Only the continuist urge
... can represent this differential as representing labor, even if "labor" is
taken to imply "as objectified in the commodity". (1987: 158)

In the present juncture Spivak highlights the role of computers as one of the more serious manifestations of the unequal relations of productive forces between the two worlds, in particular the role of computers as providing a massive impetus to production in the first world. The still insignificant presence of computers in the other world thus further helps extend the reach of multinational corporatism there and facilitate information retrieval. Given this scenario, her argument runs, the conflation of labour with value elides the differences in labour-producing value in first-world production compared to that in the third world. The substantiality and continuing, if not increasing, power of multinational capital rests on third world labour. There is an "out-valuing" of first world productivity at the same time that third world productivity is appropriated. This is accompanied by the dismantling of the "nationalist" predication of value:

It is a paradox that capitalist humanism does indeed tacitly make its plans by the "materialist" predication of Value, even as its official ideology offers the discourse of humanism as such; while Marxist cultural studies in the First World cannot ask the question of Value within the "materialist" predication of the subject, since the question would compel one to acknowledge that the text of exploitation might implicate Western cultural studies in the international division of labour. (166)

What implications does this have for her stance on the canon? She stresses the need for oppositional canons as they emerge from histories of domination and help to heal the wounds of such domination. But she is too well aware that the debate around canonicity is more often than not carried out within the "idealist" structure of epistemology. "Concentrating on the desire for the canon, on the complicity with old standards, and on epistemic violence", she argues, "the practical perspective of the discipline in the narrow sense need do no more than persistently clean up (or muddy) the "idealist" field as it nourishes the question of value" (155). Under conditions

dictated by advanced industrial capital, what her labour highlights is the structure of organization that, in the first place,
set up the possibility of canon-formation. She does not provide us with a list of norms that would guide us to this end.
What she does is to strategically advocate the reading of
canonical texts with other local language texts (see also Mahood 1977) to problematize the construction of the implied
reader.

It would be wrong to impute any consistently faithful theoretical position to Spivak. MacCabe in his 'Foreword' to her
book refers to this when he says that she is "often called a
feminist Marxist deconstructionist" (1987: ix). She is interested in the stresses and strains of speaking from any given, and
thus necessarily implicating, location, thus making a virtue of
her own positionality. Robert Young probably has this in mind
when he suggests that the rigorous engagement of her work is
"best approached not through critical or historical labels, but
in terms of the politico-theoretical difficulties which it raises"
(1990: 158). Her mix of feminism, Marxism, and deconstruction is mainly deployed in analysing the silencing of the
Other, particularly the native subaltern woman. While doing
this, she is not arguing for a recuperation of the voice of the
subaltern but rather a fundamental questioning of methods
used by critics. To the critic's investigation of the processes of
subject-constitution as subalterns must be added, if not priori-
tised, the inevitable subject effects of any critical practice
(including mine).

Spivak warns against a critical practice that can be easily
entrapped in a sort of "reverse-ethnocentrism" when engaging in a critique of imperialism. To harbour the thought that
"a critique of imperialism", as she argues in her essay 'The
Rani of Sirmur', "would restore the sovereignty for the lost
self of the colonies so that Europe could, once and for all, be
put in the place of the other that it always was" (1985a: 128)
is at best a nostalgic act. Whether it is the subversive native
critic or the well-intentioned western scholar, an attitude

towards the native of "hyperbolic admiration ... or pious guilt" (1988: 299) can only be counter-productive. The project of recovering the native elements of culture can only draw upon the terms set by the colonizing power that has constructed the other in its own likeness.

An awareness of one's imbrication in this sort of knowledge production, a relentless questioning of hegemonic forms, a conscious unlearning of the paralyzing norms and undoing of the structures and the systems within which the oppositional critic has to operate, becomes for Spivak the task and responsibility of a liberating critical praxis. It is in the context of these kinds of formulations that the existing form and practice of English studies in India appears to be irrelevant. A need to be critically aware about literature (in this case English literature) as production thus becomes all the more imperative for readers inhabiting postcolonial spaces. And it is this line of thought, which I will take up in my conclusion, that suggests the replacement of English studies by a more enabling and responsive discipline such as a critical historical and cultural studies.

BHABHA: INTERSTITIAL RESISTANCE

The legitimizing postulate of colonialist discourse, in Bhabha's formulation, is the notion of 'time-lag', that of extending the project of modernization to areas outside the West. The non-West, through this catalystic intervention, is meant to quickly evolve from the state of nature to that of culture, and become a mirror-image of its benefactor. But, of course, such a state of affairs would render the whole project nonsensical, because it will erase all distinctions between the West and the rest. The categories which divide the 'first' from the 'third' world would dissolve; the non-West in its transformation would have become a clone of the West.

In the discursive arrangement that colonialism constructs, the tutelage and responsibility for this mission is Europe's. As the only continent that has named itself, it is recumbent upon it to draw from its *inherent* genius in supplying the uplift for those seen as less endowed.[15] This agenda that colonialism sets up for itself, Bhabha evinces, places it in an embarrassingly paradoxical position. Only by reducing the specificity of its essential genius, or by self-deconstruction, can the project of modernity for the darker races bear fruit. This split at the enunciatory site of colonialist logic, according to Bhabha, results in a discourse and social formation marked with a kind of perversion described by Fanon as 'Manichean delirium'. Bhabha explains:

The representative figure of such a perversion ... is the image of post-Enlightenment man tethered to, not confronted by, his dark reflection, the shadow of colonized man that splits his presence, distorts his outline, breaches his boundaries, repeats his actions at a distance, disturbs and divides the very time of his being. (1986: xiv)

The colonizer and the colonized are bound together in the logic of a necessary hierarchy. The self-designed mission cannot take off unless the very grounds of that hierarchy are dismantled. A discourse that is sutured so viscerally with contradiction has to rely on the absolute ardour of its enunciatory will. The repeated avowals of humanism and civility are actually made to stick by assumed power. The organization of space in the colony reveals all:

The barracks stand by the church which stands by the schoolroom; the cantonment stands hard by the "civil lines". Such visibility of the institutions and apparatuses of power is possible because the exercise of colonial power makes their *relationship* obscure, produces them as fetishes, spectacles of a "natural"/racial pre-eminence. Only the seat of government is always elsewhere – alien and separate by that distance upon which surveillance depends for its strategies of objectification, normalisation and discipline. (Bhabha 1983: 35)

To closely scrutinize the language of colonialism is thus to recognise the play of power even as the erosion of its cognitive ratiocination proceeds apace.

What bearing does this have on the postcolonial formation? The seeds of an oppositional discourse are already present in the colonial theatre and its discursive power-play. This, Bhabha demonstrates, can be made to work to provide a real advance, a true *post*ness in postcolonial discourse.[16] The rhetoric at work at the scene of colonial administration and the exercise of authority there uncovers a terrain, a productive space for such an oppositional postcolonial stance:

In order to understand the productivity of colonial power it is crucial to construct its regime of "truth", not to subject its representations to a normalizing judgement. Only then does it become possible to understand the productive ambivalence of the object of colonial discourse – that "otherness" which is at once an object of desire and derision, an articulation of difference contained within the fantasy of origin and identity. What such a reading reveals are the boundaries of colonial discourse and it enables a transgression of those limits from the space of that otherness. (1983: 19)

To further his reading of the fissures immanent in colonial discourse, Bhabha develops the celebrated notion of 'mimicry'. The normalization of the colonized subject as a "mimic man", he argues, brings to the fore once again the contradictory inbuilt mechanism of colonial discourse. The native is to be Anglicized but not turned into an English clone: "not white/not quite":

The line of descent of the mimic man can be traced through the works of Kipling, Forster, Orwell, Naipaul, and to his emergence, most recently … as the anomalous Bipin Chandra Pal. He is the effect of a flawed colonial mimesis, in which to be Anglicised is *emphatically* not to be English. (1984a: 128)[17]

The contradiction arising out of such a "flawed colonial mimesis" also becomes the occasion for a subversive move. The closer the mimic man resembles the colonizer the greater the potential for a transgression of authority:

it is as if the very emergence of the 'colonial' is dependent for its representation upon some strategic limitation or prohibition *within* the authoritative discourse itself. The success of colonial appropriation depends on a proliferation of inappropriate objects that ensure its strategic failure, so that mimicry is at once *resemblance* and *menace*. (127)
... The *menace* of mimicry is its double vision which in disclosing the ambivalence of colonial discourse also disrupts its authority. (129)

From this location of counter-insurgency, two possible readings emerge. The first suggests that the figure of the mimic man is a retroactive descriptive model which emerges from Bhabha's interpretation of a determinate moment in colonialism and its enunciation. The second possibility is that of finding in it an atemporal undermining moment that extends in its reach to the neocolonial formation as well.

The first reading goes as far as pointing out the significance of dissimulated power and ambivalence in the exercise of colonial authority and the importance of drawing this lesson from history. The more consequential suggestion leads to seeing colonialism's mimic man as always-already undermining colonialist supremacy from within even in the neocolonial régime. Bhabha's positing of the mode wherein the West, as a fallout of colonialism, is necessarily "tethered to" the non-West indicates how the once colonized societies perforce become "dark shadows" of their erstwhile colonizer, shadows that replicate the conduct of that colonizer at a distance.

This model has the explanatory power of showing up the inevitable ills ailing the political structures, institutions, and mindsets in contemporary postcolonial societies which are fashioned after the prototypical West that has no 'such' problems any more. What this points to, perhaps, is the potency of the Dependency Theory argument advanced by André Gunder Frank, Immanuel Wallerstein and others, and the more sophisticated economic dependency model formulated by Samir Amin. Despite their divergences, these economic world-views imply that the postcolonial nation-state is bound to a global system which perpetuates its marginalization. Focusing on the nation-state and the incorporation of the periphery economies into the world capitalist order, Frank finds hierarchical relations between the two Worlds responsible for preventing the effective possibility of sustained, dynamic capitalist development for the periphery. Integration into the global economy came about through an intermediate metropolis-satellite chain, wherein the surplus generated at every stage progressively accrued to the centre. The most underdeveloped nations are consequently those with the strongest ties in the past. Throughout the various stages of capitalism – mercantilist, industrial, and financial – a certain kind of exchange relationship is seen to have remained constant. Ernesto Laclau characterizes this as "a) a system of production for the market, in which b) profit constitutes the motive of production, and c) this profit is realized for the benefit of someone other than the direct producer, who is thereby dispossessed of it" (1971: 24-25). Laclau's critique of Frank stresses the primacy of the conditions of production over those of exchange. Underdeveloped countries should be understood, according to him, in terms of the system of relations between the capitalist and non-capitalist modes of production, instead of Frank's homogeneous capitalist relations.

Amin goes further still by combining the world capitalist system with a theory of unequal exchange to explain blocked development in the periphery. A core and a periphery exist at all the stages of development that he lists: mercantilist, premonoply/competitive, and monoply/imperialist. The dichotomy, according to him, hardens in the imperialist stage when no country of the periphery or semiperiphery is able to join the core: "I maintain that the dynamic of the core is

autonomous, that the periphery adjusts to it, and that the functions the periphery fulfils differ from one stage to another"
(1982: 168-69).

This raises questions about that aspect of Bhabha's formulation which privileges subversion as that which is always
already there. The whole notion of economic dependency in
the double time of modernity simulates mimicry, but the
translation from a psychic model to a socio-economic one is, at
best, a difficult task. An explication of how this interrelationship works or might work is not made available but the strain
is a recurring theme in most of his work. In his 'Foreword' to
Fanon's *Black Skin, White Masks*, Bhabha writes:

He [Fanon] may yearn for a total transformation of Man and Society,
but he speaks most effectively from the uncertain interstices of historical change: from the area of ambivalence between race and sexuality:
out of an unresolved contradiction between culture and class; from deep
within the struggle of *psychic representation* and *social reality*. (1986:
ix; emphases added)

Here we have the clearest articulation of the tension that characterizes Fanon's work. Bhabha's preferences are for those
moments when Fanon speaks "from the uncertain interstices
of historical change". The yearning for "a total transformation
of Man and Society" is a dream that cannot be chased; it reeks
of "an existential humanism that is as banal as it is beatific"
(xx).

Commenting on Bhabha's recuperation of Fanon, Henry
Louis Gates Jr. observes that "Bhabha may be Fanon's closest
reader, and it is an oddly touching performance of a coaxing
devotion: he regrets aloud those moments in Fanon that cannot be reconciled to the poststructuralist critique of identity
because he wants Fanon to be even better than he is" (1991:
460). Gates goes on to say that Bhabha "wants Fanon to mean
Lacan rather than, say, Jean-Paul Sartre, but he acknowledges
that Fanon does tend to slip" (461).

It is in Fanon's slippage – the attempt to see the social in terms of the psychic – that Bhabha locates the limitations of his formulations:

> he turns too hastily from the ambivalences of identification to the an-tagonistic identities of political alienation and cultural discrimination; he is too quick to name the Other, to personalize its presence in the lan-guage of colonial racism ... These attempts, in Fanon's words, *to restore the dream to its proper political time and cultural space* can, at times blunt the edge of Fanon's brilliant illustrations of the complexity of psy-chic projections in the pathological colonial relation. (1986: xix-xx; em-phasis added)

In his efforts to articulate the pathologies of colonialism, Fanon resorts to a Freudianism unhappily sitting with a sort of Sartrean Marxism. But the force of his avowal issues from the immediacies of the political moment, rather than the con-sistencies of his conceptual framework. (This, of course, is true of any writer or text from a cultural studies perspective.) "In his more analytic mode", Bhabha writes, "Fanon can impede the exploration of [...] ambivalent, uncertain questions of colonial desire. The state of emergency from which he writes demands more insurgent answers, more immediate identifica-tions" (xix).

How much of a theory can be raised by a structure of ideas in the determinate moment? Fanon, as Gates observes, "is a battlefield in himself" (1991). The task of reading him is thus circumscribed by "an acknowledgement of his own historical particularity, as an actor whose own search for self-transcend-ence scarcely exempts him from the heterogeneous and con-flictual structures that we have taken to be characteristic of colonial discourse" (470). But for Bhabha, this is clearly not enough. As he sees it, Fanon's slips are signs of a surplus zeal. The "purveyor of the transgressive and the transitional truth" (ix) does not live up to his promise:

It is as if Fanon is fearful of his most radical insights: that the space of the body and its identification is a representational reality; that the politics of race will not be entirely contained within the humanist myth of man or economic necessity or historical progress, for its psychic effects question such forms of determinism. (1986: xx)

Bhabha thus rules out dialectic closure and instead invests in the notion of culture as a dialogic condition of struggle.

His essay 'Freedom's Basis in the Indeterminate', is an attempt to formulate this notion of culture which reconfigures the social. Questions of political community, he shows, go beyond the nation-space:

Postcolonial perspectives emerge from the colonial or anticolonialist testimonies of Third World countries and from the testimony of minorities within the geopolitical division of East/West, North/South. These perspectives intervene in the ideological discourses of modernity that have attempted to give a hegemonic 'normality' to the uneven development and the differential, often disadvantaged, histories of nations, races, communities, and peoples. Their critical revisions are formulated around issues of cultural difference, social authority, and political discrimination in order to reveal the antagonistic and ambivalent moments within the "rationalizations" of modernity. (1992: 46)

The discourse of cultural difference, in his view, demands a total revision of "social *temporality*" (46) such that

the affective experience of social marginality – as it emerges in noncanonical cultural forms – transforms our critical strategies. It forces us to confront the concept of culture outside *objets d'art* or beyond the canonization of the "Idea" of aesthetics, and thus to engage with culture as an uneven, incomplete production of meaning and value, often composed of incommensurable demands and practices, and produced in the act of social survival. (47)

Whereas the conception of culture consecrated in the canon relies on the division of the globe and the division between 'high' and 'low',

[t]he transmission of "cultures" of survival does not occur in the ordered *musee ordinaire* of national cultures – with their claims to the continuity of an authentic past and a living present – regardless of whether this scale of value is preserved in the organicist national traditions of romanticism or within the more universal proportions of classicism. (47)

INDIANIST PROVOCATION

Very little has been written about the work of Spivak or Bhabha in India. The occasional acknowledgement that appears in print often takes the form of an outright dismissal. The charge most commonly made is that their writings are too theoretical and elitist. Thus, Suvir Kaul describes Bhabha as "a privileged spokesman for a 'Third World' position" (1992: 221).

The reason for this animosity lies partly in the uneasy relationship that the average Indian academic appears to have with 'theory', especially poststructuralism, and partly in righteous notions of "intellectual nationalism".[18] About the latter line of argument, Makarand Paranjape explains: "By nationalism I have in mind concepts like *Swatantra*, *Swarajya*, and *Swadharma*; but a more appropriate expression for intellectual nationalism might perhaps be Swadeshi – home-made" (1989: 81). This mode of opposition is not a move toward fashioning an 'intermediate technology' suitable for the 'Less Developed Countries'. It is a response consequent on fear: "On marches Logos, constructing, deconstructing, reconstructing – coiling and uncoiling itself, python-like. We, the marginalized, neo-colonials watch with profound awe – that is, until we discover that we are in the belly of the python" (77). Paranjape calls for the generation of counter-colonial discourses and has no patience for the India-born intellectual situated in the West:

[B]y choosing to live and work in the West and by using the benefits of its system, such an intellectual forfeits, at least partially, her or his right to speak on our behalf. Only those who live and work in and for the third world, strictly speaking, have this right. That is, by merely living in the third world, sharing its day to day struggle for selfhood and dignity, an intellectual participates and thus represents this struggle; the expatriate intellectual, on the other hand, best represents his own cause, but unless he has been forced into exile, may not be accepted as the voice of his people. It is given to the former type of intellectual to build the counter-imperialistic discourse. Our expatriate brothers and sisters who have settled down in the West are really fighting for themselves, not for us. They are fighting for their own survival with all they have got. For them their ethnicity or colonial background becomes a pretext, a handle by which they can manipulate the system which would otherwise finish them. We can give them our sympathy and support but not the authority of speaking on our behalf. Their concern is with finding a legitimate place for themselves within the West, while our struggle is with finding an *alternative* to it. (1989: 78)

This kind of polemic is riddled with problems, not least in that it homogenises both the third world and the metropolis. (Ironically, in suggesting that post-colonial intellectuals in the West are "fighting for their own survival", the polemic confers on them a certain degree of intellectual heroism.) On a more serious note, though, it does not allow us to raise the question whether there are no alternatives to the West in the West and vice versa. Clearly, being in India guarantees neither a 'metropolitan-free' standpoint nor an unproblematic relation to the material there-ness of some indigenous culture. Furthermore, in response to the issue of the right "to speak on our behalf", the postcolonial theorist might respond that s/he speaks for nobody.[19]

Finally, the critique falls short on its own terms: the critic does not say what the alternative to postcolonial or any other critical discourse originating in Western academe might be. Apart from vague references to "Indian theories of meaning and interpretation" and their native progenitors – "Bharata, Nagarjuna, Anandavardhana, Abhinavagupta" – there is little effort to engage with the indigenous tradition or what the latter can legitimately offer.[20] The irony is that the Indian teacher of English (and modern Indian literatures) in the university has, more often than not, little access to the ancient Sanskrit traditions of poetics.

In what might appear as a similar attack on the notion of the 'postcolonial', Arif Dirlik points an accusing finger at Spivak and Bhabha (among others) for being Third World intellectuals ensconced in the groves of First World academe (1994: 329). But more importantly, he charges that postcolonial theory neglects to think of the economic dimension of the cultural. Dirlik is not entirely right in arguing that this dimension of the pervasiveness of global capitalism is ignored; but he is right in so far as there is no *direct* engagement with it. This lacuna, in what is otherwise a useful way of looking at our world, can perhaps be developed, especially as scholars worldwide are taking increasing cognizance of it (see Hall 1996).

In explicating the positions (in as much as one can explicate shifting positions) of Spivak and Bhabha, I have tried to tease out an agenda that might be useful in looking at English studies in India. Thus, Bhabha's avowal of 'noncanonical cultural forms' which express 'social marginality', of culture as process, and Spivak's attempts to bring in the politico-economic in the realm of cultural production and consumption, opens up legitimate spaces for the study of popular culture. Located with the rubric of a critical historical and cultural studies, this kind of academic endeavour is what this book is making a case for.

Notes

1   A writer in *The New York Times*, for instance, says that the revival
    of colonialism "is a trend that should be encouraged ... on practical
    as well as moral grounds. There simply is no alternative in nations
    where governments have crumbled and the most basic conditions
    for civilized life have disappeared, as is now the case in a great many
    third-world countries" (Johnson 1993: 22). And further, that "the
    civilized world has a mission to go to these desperate places and
    govern". "The only satisfaction", for the civilized, "will be the un-
    spoken gratitude of millions of misgoverned or ungoverned people
    who will find in this altruistic revival of colonialism the only way
    out of their present intractable miseries"(44).

2   I am indebted to David Johnson's unpublished paper for this refer-
    ence.

3   Athough Coomarswamy was one of the finest expounders of East-
    ern aesthetics, his limitations, as Partha Mitter has written, "arose
    from the fact that even he ultimately fell back upon European
    standards for evaluating Indian art" (1977: 285). Coomarswamy,
    Mitter shows, insisted "that a genuine *swadeshi* outlook was the
    only alternative to colonialism" (1994: 261). *Swadeshi* protest was
    "a spiritual struggle against an alien ideal. Artists with their deeper
    sense of political wrongs and their longing for self-realisation were
    the true nation-builders. Coomarswamy took to task the political
    activists for their indifference to Indian art while they condemned
    Curzon. Curzon, he reminded them, had shown more concern for
    the national heritage than they ever did" (261).

4   In the realm of Shakespeare criticism, later Indian critics have been
    content to dwell on Aristotelian ideas of plot and characterisation:
    P.C. Ghosh's *Shakespeare's Mingled Drama* (1960), S.C. Sen Gupta's
    Aspects of Shakespearean Tragedy (1972), Alur Janakiram's *Reason
    and Love in Shakespeare: A Selective Study* (1977) are all marked by
    their inability to relate it in any way to the Indian context.

5   Charu Sheel Singh (1989), *The Literary Criterion* 23, 4 (14-26).

6   Jasbir Jain (1989), *Rajasthan University Studies In English*, 1 (61-69).

7   Needless to say, the assumption that there was no theory before

structuralism or poststructuralism arrived on the scene can hardly be taken seriously. Williams remarks in his essay 'Crisis of English studies', that literary critics who claimed to be above all 'isms', hardly ever put to scrutiny the 'ism' of their own criticism (1983).

8 The story reenacts the peasant uprising of Naxalbari in the late sixties which was ruthlessly suppressed both by the Central and the West Bengal provincial government. For a detailed analysis of the rebellion see Sankar Ghosh's *The Naxalite Movement: A Maoist Experiment* (1974).

9 Bruce Robbins makes a similar point when he translates Disraeli's famous observation about the East being a career into the "Third world is a career" in contemporary times (1993: 152).

10 In an interview Spivak says, "I don't have a problem with something being a contradiction. I think contradictions can be productive" (1990: 127). The relation between ideology-critique and deconstuction in her mind is also not entirely resolved despite her insistence to the contrary: "The problem with the idea of decon-struction as a form of ideology-critique is that deconstruction is not really interested in the exposure of error … . Derrida is interested in how truth is constructed rather than in exposing error … . Deconstruction can only speak in the language of the thing it critic-ises. So as Derrida says, it falls prey to its own critique, *in a certain way*. That makes it very different from ideology-critique" (1990: 135; emphases in the original). As Rey Chow argues, "her use of de-construction can indeed be seen as a form of ideology critique (as for instance the critique of "first world" imperialism) that is in keeping with the reconstructive and reinventive spirit of the Enlightenment. *There is nothing wrong with such a use*, but there is a problem". Also "if deconstruction is, as Spivak says, not inter-ested in the exposure of error, where does her ethical charge come from?" (1993: 8).

11 For an explanation of catachreses see 'Poststructuralism, Marginal-ity, Post-coloniality, and Value', note 20, pp. 241-42. She speaks of catachreses in *The Postcolonial Critic* more directly: "A deconstruc-tive awareness would insistently be aware that the master-words are catachreses … that there are no literal referents, there are no

'true' examples of the 'true worker', the 'true woman', the 'true proletarian'" (1990: 104).

12 Ideology seen this way would lead one to approve of symptomatic reading. Spivak is not too keen on such readings because the assumption here is of a structure consisting of analyst and analysand which harks back to the problem of the science-ideology opposition in Althusser's formulations.

13 In an interview with Young, Spivak responds to the case of an Indian research student who wants to write his thesis on deconstruction in Anglo-America. There is an unmistakable feeling of unease about how 'reverential' such a project seems and also of theory working in a neo-colonial way (1991: 234).

14 Marx develops this account in the first volume of *Capital*.

15 That Europe is singular in naming itself is an idea that Derrida alluded to in his talk at the University of Sussex, July 1993.

16 In *The Location of Culture* Bhabha makes clear his enabling notion of the 'post': it is not to "indicate sequentiality" (1994: 4) but our living on "the borderlines of the 'present'", "the moment of transit where space and time cross to produce complex figures of difference and identity, past and present, inside and outside, inclusion and exclusion" (1).

17 Bhabha here simply renders, albeit with the adjective 'anomalous', Bipin Chandra Pal as the most recent example of the mimic man. Benedict Anderson has used the case of Pal (with a reading of his memoirs) to point to the successful operation of Macaulay's project. A more informed reading of Pal, the fiery leader of the Swadeshi movement in Bengal, suggests that his language is "indicative of the very real imbrication of two discourses, and correspondingly of two domains, of politics", that of 'elite' and 'subaltern' politics (Chatterjee 1993: 12).

18 For C.D. Narasimhaiah, the revival of interest in traditional Indian poetics is "a counterblast to the newer theories of structuralism and deconstructionism". In the predictable manner of nationalist critics, he invokes the name of a western critic to defend a nostalgic return to the invented/rediscovered Sanskrit traditions. Thus, "Susanne Langer remarked that all the pleasures of heaven and earth were not

equal to a little of what *rasa* (aesthetic experience of an emotion) could give" (1993: 19). He lambasts, "The critical theorist who made a mystique of imported critical theories which had their origin in France where they were wisely forgotten while they continued to rage fiercely in the United States, thanks to its faith in 'Make it new'. Such were structuralism, post-structuralism and deconstructionism. It became fashionable in Indian universities to loftily mouth cliches like 'The death of the author' and to ask 'Is there a reader?' and worse, 'Is there a text?'" (22).

19 "I never speak 'for' anybody": Homi Bhabha in a private conversation with the author.

20 That is not to say that there are no attempts at recovering/reworking such theories from Indian poetics and aesthetics. See, for example, Krishna Rayan's 'The Case for an Indian Poetic Based on the Dhvani Theory'. His claim is that Dhvani theory of Anandavardhana and Abhnivagupta in "[i]ts formulation of the nature and status of suggested meaning (*vyangyartha*) in relation to the other two tiers – metaphorical meaning (*laksyartha*) and stated meaning (*vacyartha*) – has a unique across-the-board applicability in the interpretation of literary texts" (1984: 41).

CHAPTER TWO

'Our Commerce Will Follow'
Englishing India

*Was Kim going to school? Then he, an MA of Calcutta Univer-
sity, would explain the advantages of education. There were
marks to be gained by due attention to Latin and Wordsworth's
Excursion (all this was Greek to Kim). Also a man might go far,
as he himself had done, by strict attention to plays called Lear
and Julius Caesar, both much in demand by examiners on the
Bengal side.*

Rudyàrd Kipling 1994: 152

This chapter will delineate some of the dominant historical
and political forces that made the installation of English as the
official language in colonial India imperative. Some of the repercussions of this education policy will also be suggested. The
issue of 'English' in the postcolonial 'nation' – in the same
way as, say, parliamentary democracy – is not, I argue, just a
question of legacy, but one of constitutive determinations.

Let us begin with Nicholas Dirks's warning that any effort
to "make a systematic statement about the colonial project
runs the risk of denying the fundamental historicity of colonialism, as well as conflating cause and effect". It is

tempting but wrong to ascribe either intentionality or systematicity to
a congeries of activities and a conjunction of outcomes that, though

related and at times co-ordinated, were usually diffuse, disorganised and even contradictory. (1992: 7)

While Dirks's caution is well taken, it does not necessarily contradict the idea of constitutive determinations. Just as it would be inane to assert the discursive unity of colonialism, it would be facile to disavow a project that was successful enough to enable us to speak of a system of representations and practices. Thus, the historical transition from colonisation to decolonisation can be better thought of as a non-Hegelian reconfiguration where old elements survive to exercise considerable after-effects. The new ensemble, in this sense, is a more dynamic notion than that of legacy.

Despite the 'diffuse', disorganised' and sometimes 'contradictory' nature of activities and effects, a certain degree of "systematicity" is inevitable in a thetic project and my argument will at times suffer from it. It is a truism now to say that every beginning and method, every discourse involves exclusion. As Foucault has indicated:

The question posed by language analysis of some discursive fact or another is always: according to what rules has a particular statement been made, and consequently according to what rules could other similar statements be made? The description of the events of discourse poses a quite different question: how is it that one particular statement appeared rather than another? (1972: 27)

The problem of seeing beginnings as "specific events" or "abstractions" and the problem of human agency will haunt my project. As Edward Said puts it:

If a field of knowledge comprises a wide-ranging array of "events" governed by impersonal rules; if this field cannot be rationally understood in terms of the genetic concepts formerly exemplified by heroes, founding fathers, continuous temporal narratives, and divine ordinance; and if nevertheless the field is universal, that is, if it involves the individual human regardless of will, by means of applying such notions as class, mind, pattern, structure, history, or evolution – if all of these, then what power is left to the individual freely to act, to intervene, to motivate, when he wishes to effect a rational beginning for a course or project in that field? (1985: 52)

What I aim for is a kind of productive anxiety between the two terms of the problematic – on the one hand, "specific events" and "abstractions", and on the other "determinations" and "specificities", such that a situation of dialogism emerges.

'The Vilest Interests'[1]

British residence in India was formally codified on December 31, 1600 when Queen Elizabeth I granted trade monopoly to the East India Company. By 1615 the Company had four trading posts, and by 1647 the number had gone up to twenty-three. Although the Company was initially one of many rival European powers operating in India, by the middle of the eighteenth century it had become practically the master of Bengal. In 1765 it obtained the *Diwani* (or the financial control) of Bengal, Bihar and Orissa, declaring its readiness, "to stand forth as Diwan", and by the agency of the Company servants, "to take upon themselves the entire management of revenues" (Hastings 1841: 214).

From a 'mercantile/warrior' institution (Washbrook 1981), the East India Company began to appropriate governmental responsibility and substitute the pre-colonial state with a statecraft of its own making. This development of the principles of statecraft relied on two essential considerations. First, to extract economic surplus from the agrarian economy by way of revenue. Second, to ensure political control while engaging militarily as little as possible. Setting up the rule of law and property right laws was among the main axioms of this statecraft as can be read in the Permanent Settlement of 1793.

Quoting from Eric Stokes' paper, 'The rationale of British Indian Empire, 1826-56', C.A. Bayly notes:

By 1818 the Indian revenues in British hands amounted to some £22 million. They were used to cover the large deficit on Britain's balance of trade with both India and China. First, there were large unreciprocated transfers of bullion and bills from India to Britain which were known as the Home Charges. This was the prime component of what the nationalist historians were to term as the 'drain of wealth'. With the salaries and fortunes also transferred the total amounted by 1820 to £6 million annually. (1988: 116)

With an economic interest of such massive proportions, the need for clinging on to India is not difficult to understand. But colonialism is not just a matter of raw-material exports and manufactured goods imports; or, more generally, the subordination and control of the colonial economy to the economy of the imperialist centre. "Economic exploitation," Viswanathan argues, "required the sanction of higher motives" (1989: 164). The instrumentality of English literature was one such source that supplied higher motives. "The split between the material and discursive practices of colonialism is nowhere sharper", points out Viswananthan, "than in the progressive rarefaction of the rapacious, exploitative, and ruthless actor of history into the reflexive subject of literature" (1987: 23).

Although the British presence on Indian territory, as noted earlier, went back to the late sixteenth century, English achieved official language status only in the mid-nineteenth century. Charles Grant's proposal of 1792 that English be made the language of instruction at all levels became an actuality on March 7, 1835. Lord Bentick, the Governor General in Council, passed a brief resolution for the "promotion of European literature and science among the natives of India". The Minute made English the medium of instruction in government-subsidised schools and, in effect, the official language of British India. The rationale put forward at the time was de-

rived from the hugely influential view of the utilitarian James
Mill who found nations such as India "tainted with the vices
of insincerity" and "dissembling, treacherous, mendacious to
an excess which surpasses even the unusual measure of uncultivated society" (quoted in Kopf 1980: 504).

The decision to promote English and the study of English
literature in India was a result of a network of configurations,
but was primarily determined by the pressing need for an effective strategy of containment (Ahmad 1987). Though there
was a protracted debate over issues of language and the mode
of instruction, the specific appeal of western education was
twofold. First, to help maintain and consolidate British supremacy in India (which was of paramount importance to the pol-
icy-makers) and secondly, to act as a palisade against "the
proneness of the period to movements subversive to the established order of things" (Marshman in Sinha 1964: 5). Of all
the interpellating apparatuses or regimes of truth, western
secular education was seen by the British administration as
the most convenient and effective means of establishing "the
foundation for a stability that 'even a political revolution will
not destroy and upon which after many ages may rest a vast
superstructure'" (from the 1826 *Asiatic Journal,* cited in Viswanathan 1989: 117).[2]

'The Necessary Furniture of Empire'

The transformation, with the Diwani in 1765, from a mercan-
tile power to a revenue-collecting agency was of great import.
The trading organisation in effect became the sovereign power
in Bengal. Warren Hastings, the Governor-General from 1774
to 1785, was faced with the job of organising an elaborate
bureaucracy as the maintenance of law and order gradually
entered the purview of the Company's activities in addition to
revenue assessment and collection. Hastings remonstrated ac-
ridly in his letters to Company directors about the ineptitude
of the Company servants and implored them for the induction

of a training programme. His aim was to produce a service of orientalized elites, well versed in Indian languages and responsive to local traditions and customs. This presumed equation between acculturation and administrative efficiency provided the *raison d'être* for Hastings' enthusiasm for understanding Indian culture.

The pragmatic side of his orientalism was in turn reinforced by his admiration of Indian cultural heritage. His orientalism was that of "positive geography and history" as opposed to "imaginative geography and history" (Said 1979: 55). The cultural relativism that he brought to bear on his project is evident from his comments on *The Bhagavat-Geeta*:

Might I, an unlettered man, venture to prescribe bounds to the latitude of criticism, *I should exclude, in estimating the merit of such a production, all rules from the ancient or modern literature of Europe,* all references to such sentiments or manners as are become the standards of propriety for opinion and action in our modes of life, and equally all appeals to our revealed tenets of religion, and moral duty. I should exclude them, as by no means applicable to the language, sentiments, manners, or morality appertaining to a system of society with which we have been for ages unconnected, and of an antiquity preceding even the first efforts of civilisation in our own Quarter of the globe, which, in respect to the general diffusion and common participation of arts and sciences, may now be considered as one community. (quoted in Marshall 1970: 185; emphasis added)

Hastings showed no inclination to interfere in 'native' affairs and worked predominantly through the existing governmental machinery. The replacement of Hindu and Muslim legal systems by English law was unacceptable to him and explains his patronage of oriental scholarship. Besides, Hastings was opposed to the extension of British law (under the Regulating Act of 1773) to Indians as well as the Company employees because he also "regarded the Supreme Court as a possible threat to his own freedom of government and a rival to the

Company's own system of policing" (Musselwhite 1986: 83).
His encouragement of the study of Islamic and Hindu codes of
law coincided with the British Parliament's increasing alarm at
the 'depravity' of the administrators and merchants in these
far-flung shores. As Edmund Burke[3] remarked, the British
government was motivated to "form a strong and solid security for the natives against oppression of British subjects resident in Bengal" (Stokes 1959: 2).

But the paradox of Hastings' position is that the idea of codifying 'Hindu' and 'Muslim' law *was* realised during his time
and proved a significant intervention. Law in pre-colonial India
was not a fixed, immutable body of knowledge (Derrett 1968).
The Warren Hastings Plan of 1772 (which was later to become
The Administration of Justice Regulation of April 11th, 1780)
proclaimed that the *sastris* (learned pundits of Hindu law)
would be consulted on matters relating to caste, religious
usages, marriage, etc. (Derrett 1968: 232-33). Thus began the
project of codifying Hindu (and later Muslim) law by British
administrators and jurists with the help of local pundits. This
patronage of the *sastras* was further embodied in the founding
of the Sanskrit College at Benaras and in Calcutta. This nexus
with the *sastris* ensured that a more Brahmanical mode em-
phasising the immutability of native religious axioms, was imposed on the native society (Cohn 1987). Validation of the caste
system and the *varna* theory of social order were also thus
carried out. Those groups who had hitherto existed outside
the sphere of the Brahmanical precepts were thus made subjects of its scriptural dictates (Washbrook 1981; Cohn 1987).
Domination was deeply inscribed within pre-colonial India
and colonialism, for its own purposes, helped, but not without
a significant reconstitution, reinforce it.

Philip Francis, a rival of Hastings and member of the
Supreme Council in Bengal set up under the Regulating Act of
1773, wanted to impose "Enlightenment and European principles of political economy on India" by transforming the
zemindars into functionaries in the manner of English

squires.[4] In contrast, Hastings was concerned to "manipulate as best as he could the residual machinery of the Mughal Empire". Musselwhite cites Michael Edwardes' suggestion that "British Oriental scholarship originated in the need to counterbalance the effects of the introduction into India of British judicial processes" (1986: 83).

The British political position was far from consolidated, and Hastings desperately sought to win over the governed. "[E]very accumulation of knowledge and especially such as is obtained by social communication with people over whom we exercise a dominion founded on the right of conquest," wrote Hastings in a letter to Nathaniel Smith, Chairman of the Court of Directors, "is useful to the state; it is the gain of humanity" (Kopf 1969: 18). Colonial knowledge was inextricably bound with power (Cohn 1985) but to attribute positive design to all of Hastings' efforts in the encouragement of oriental scholarship is not only unjust, but also restrictive; as Foucault has shown, power cannot be analysed in terms of conscious intentions. The dominant themselves are contained within power matrices, although their rationales are important data.

Lord Cornwallis, who succeeded Hastings as Governor General in 1786, was faced with deteriorating standards in government (including a corrupt system of administration) and serious financial problems (see Bayly 1988: 65-66).[5] His immediate challenge was the creation of efficient administrative machinery that could provide the company regular surplus revenue. Veering away from Hastings' orientalist predilections, Cornwallis strongly promoted the Europeanization of the service. Cornwallis was anxious "to make everything as English as possible in a country which resembles England in nothing" (cited in Aspinall 1931: 173). The fulcrum of the financial conundrum for Cornwallis lay in what he considered to be the official indulgence towards oriental forms of governmental organisation. "I think it must be universally admitted that without a large and well-regulated body of Europeans,

our hold of these valuable dominions must be very insecure"
(quoted in Thompson & Garrat 1958: 174).[6]

Issues of authority revolving around questions of instituted power-relations were, for Cornwallis, uppermost; and that
in his view was what faced the servants of the East India Company. It was a conviction with him that aberrant behaviour
had been caused by the adoption of a despotic form of oriental government.[7] Close contact with the natives, he argued,
had produced a general decline in morality, which had, in turn,
led to large-scale corruption among Company officials. He
therefore set himself the task of extricating Indians from important posts in the administration. It was thought that good
government could be restored by the introduction of political
principles and laws, which embodied the British system of justice.

The process of Anglicisation set in motion by Cornwallis,
however, resulted in more inflexibly defined master-subject
relations. Richard Wellesley (1798-1805) whose chief goal
seemed to be to preserve the territories acquired by the Empire, however, did not continue this policy of expediency and
caution.[8] A transformation of Indian society was not attempted, and Wellesley appeared to limit his Anglicisation to the
sphere of the government. Resolute in repressing any dissi-
dent radical thought and determined to have a body of efficient loyal administrators, he contrived a scheme for instruct-
ing recruits in Sanskrit, Persian, Arabic and other regional Indian languages; along with this it was decided that they
should be taught administrative skills, law, and history.[9] The
Fort William College founded in 1799 for this express purpose had departments of Indian languages and employed thir-
ty-three *munshis* (indigenous interpreters/clerks) who
worked in association with Orientalists like William Carey,
H.T. Colebrooke, John Gilchrist and Francis Gladwin. A sum
of approximately forty thousand rupees was set aside for the
publication of oriental literature at the college press. However, the Company directors were not happy with the

expenses that the college incurred and wanted the program to be abandoned.

John Malcolm, Thomas Munro, Charles Metcalf and Mountstuart Elphinstone, the governors who succeeded Wellesley, were all in favour of encouraging oriental scholarship. Elphinstone, for instance, in March 1824, deplored in his Minute on Education that British rule had "dried up the fountains of native talent" and that "even the actual learning of the nation" was under threat of annihilation (*Selections from the Minutes* 1884: 101-02). A notable change, however, had occurred in the fortunes of the Company, and as a consequence the orientalism of the late 1790s and early 1800s was quite different from that of the Hastings administration. For once, the British political position in India was on a much surer footing, and there was no need to court the affection of the native population. For another, none of the latter administrators shared in Hastings' enthusiasm for oriental learning and literature. As a result, the ad hocism of Hastings' policies was supplanted by more clearly articulated policies of government from 1800 onwards. At this point, policymakers began to view educational policy operatively as an ideological tool for subjugating the natives and as a means to further economic interests.[10] (See Davis and Huttenback 1987; also Viswanathan 1989). The *Fifth Report from the Select Committee on the Affairs of the East India Company* (1812) records the voices of concern at the government's "extreme unpopularity" with the buffer class of landowners who were seen as the colonial state's intermediaries with the people. The report advocates that posts in the services be reserved for the "native gentry" so that their interests are allied to those of the Company (Vol.1: 758, 769).

The Charter Act of 1813 renewed the East India Company's privileged trading status. This produced two historically significant effects: a relaxation of controls over missionary work in India, and the undertaking of responsibility by the Company state for education in India. This was enforced by the

British Parliament and was a curious occurrence since at this
stage education was not the responsibility of the state in
England. Although drawing from moral discourse, political
considerations were distinctly more important.[11]

The thirteenth resolution of the 1813 Charter stated un-
equivocally that England was responsible for promoting the
"interests and happiness" of the Indian people and that educational measures ought to be adopted "as may tend to the introduction among them of useful knowledge, and of religious
and moral improvements" (*Parliamentary Debates* 1813:
562). Section 43 of the East India Company Act of 1813 specifically set aside a lakh of rupees annually to be spent on education, "for the revival and improvement of literature ... and
for the introduction and promotion of a knowledge of the
sciences ..." (*Selections from Educational Records* 1965: 22).
This mandate triggered off an explosion of discourse around
education, in particular the debate over the implementation
and implication of the mandate, which was to be decisively
sorted out only by Lord William Bentick's 1835 resolution.

'The Best Part of the English Nation'

The future governance of India was largely debated by the
powerful lobbies of the Anglicists and the Orientalists. Although the Anglicists succeeded in bringing round the Parliament in 1835 to the view that western education would be
well-suited for India, the Orientalists' arguments for Sanskrit
and Arabic education were taken, for some time, to be persua-
sive. The Orientalists maintained that a "revival" of literature,
as inscribed in the Charter, could only refer to Sanskrit and
Arabic literature. The Anglicists converged on the term "useful learning" avowing that "it was worse than a waste of time"
to teach or be instructed in the sciences "in the state in which
they are found in the oriental books" (Trevelyan 1838: 75).

It was the fruits of oriental scholarship that paradoxically helped the Anglicists to become victors. Hastings, William Jones and their Orientalist heirs were concerned with the culture and languages of India and their ambitious explorations of the cultural legacy of the East produced an assembly of scholarship grounded in what was considered unprejudiced knowledge (Dirks 1992). If there was rediscovery as a result of Orientalism's inquiry into classical Indian history, it also fashioned a cultural past. Whatever we know of Indian history is thus entrapped in a "major contradiction" in that our "understanding of the entire Indian past" is "derived from the interpretation of Indian history made in the last two hundred years" (Thapar 1966: 3). The project for the development of the vernaculars included the production of grammars, lexicons, translations, and similar texts (cf. Dharwadker 1993; Pollock 1993). Western philology was directly embroiled in the undertaking of Orientalism. In the work of Ernest Renan, as Edward Said observes, "what comes to replace divine authority is the textual authority of the philological critic" (1983: 47). The ensemble of codified information was far from ideologically neutral; it provided material for the Anglicists' call for a transformation of premodern Indian society.

The Anglicists opposed any policy that advocated the use of native languages and literature in education as they did the hiring of native officials in any positions of power. To buttress their claims, they gestured to the failure of Hastings' administration in maintaining order. Indian traditions, it was felt, produced political dissidence and near-anarchism. Macaulay, one of the foremost Anglicists, cited the body of scholarship now available as material proof of the minor status of oriental cultures:

We have to educate a people who cannot at present be educated by means of the mother tongue. We must teach them some foreign language. The claim of our language is hardly necessary to recapitulate. It stands pre-eminent even among the languages of the west. (1952: 354)

Though formally in conflict, there was little difference between the Orientalist and Anglicist projects. Through both projects, strategies and tactics oriented toward the consolidation of power and the continuation of the colonial enterprise were manifest. Hastings, the first Orientalist administrator of note, was to defend himself thus before the House of Lords on charges of 'High Crimes and Misdemeanours' alleged to have been perpetrated during his term of office in India:

To the Commons of England, in whose name I am arraigned for desolating the provinces of their dominion in India, I dare to reply, that they are, and their representatives persist in telling them so, the most flourishing of all the States of India – it was I who made them so. The valour of others acquired, I enlarged and gave shape and consistency to the dominion which you hold there; I preserved it: I sent forth its armies with an effectual, but an economical hand, through unknown and hostile regions, to the support of your other possessions; to the retrieval of one from degradation and dishonour; and of the other, from utter loss and subjection. I maintained the wars which were of your formation, or that of others, *not of mine*. I won one member of the great Indian Confederacy from it by an act of seasonable restitution; with another I maintained a secret intercourse, and converted him into a friend; a third I threw off by diversion and negotiation, and employed him as an instrument of peace. – When you cried out for peace, and your cries were heard by those who were the object of it, I resisted this, and every other species of counteraction, by rising in my demands; and I at least afforded the efficient means by which a place, if not so durable, more seasonable at least, was accomplished with another. I gave *you all*, and you have awarded me with *confiscation, disgrace, and a life of impeachment*. (quoted in Musselwhite 1986: 91)

If Hastings advocated familiarisation of the resident British with Indian customs and the induction of Indian officials in the service, the Anglicists swore by the "spirit of English literature" in making "Indian youth" virtuous and stopping them from "regard[ing] us [as] foreigners" (Trevelyan 1838: 192). In the *Despatch to Governor-General in Council, Bengal, dated 18th February, 1824*, the Court of Directors of the Company condemned support for oriental institutions as "organically and fundamentally erroneous", deeming that the object of education is the advancement of "useful knowledge" and not "obscure and worthless knowledge" (*Selections from Educational Records* 1965: 91).

Since the identity of the colonisers could only be defined in relation to the colonised, they were both ensnared, in Bhabha's model of mimeticism, within a Lacanian mirror-image. Thus, "British civil servants in India, schooled in the 'best part of the English nation' [which for Macaulay meant English], would successfully *impress* the natives with the glories of their colonial masters ..." (Azim 1993: 13).

The Cross and the Flag

The relaxation of strictures apropos of missionary work in India was another momentous outcome of the Charter. It was not surprising that groups normally opposed to each other forged alliances in their common zeal to demonstrate that eastern religions were not, or were less, rational. Clapham Evangelists among other denominations had been frantically trying to build up a presence in India. An alliance between them and the Utilitarians and Liberals was understandable based as it was on the commonality of their eagerness to bring about a metamorphosis in the fabric of Indian civilisation. Consensus emerged on the issue and the urgent need of overhauling Indian society and, in particular, changing the 'Indian character' (see Stokes 1959).[12]

The British could not realise these goals alone without the support of indigenous forces. The effacement of the old aristocratic ruling class under Cornwallis and the ascent of the recruits of power and wealth, created a new business class who were only too keen to collaborate, and thus realised the British dream.[13] This new class derived their capital not through

inheritance but by trade with the East India Company (see
Chandra 1987-88). This located them well for purposes of
what would later be called 'filtration theory'.

This theory, which derived from the idea that cultural values percolate downwards from a site of power, was deployed
enthusiastically for dissemination by the Anglicists. The archetypal Anglicist Macaulay strategised to form an elite group
of Indians steeped in Anglocentrism who could promulgate
western philosophies and discourse. He hoped, in what is fast
becoming one of the most quoted sentences in colonial discourse, to originate a class who

may be interpreters between us and the millions whom we govern, a
class of persons Indian in blood and colour but English in taste, in opinion, in morals and intellect. (1952: 359)

Macaulay was not alone in his desire: he articulated the attitudes and opinions prevalent in the third and fourth decades
of the nineteenth century concerning the medium of instruction and curricular content.[14] Indians in places of influence and
authority, and critical of their traditions, spurred the government to displace Sanskrit education. Its persistence, wrote Raja
Rammohun Roy in a letter to William Pitt dated 11 December,
1813, would be "the best calculated to keep this country in
darkness" (Roy 1945-58, Part 4: 108).

The main preoccupation among Anglicists from the 1820s
on involved the problematic of curricular composition that
would achieve the result of creating a subject race capable of
promoting the imperial project. The curriculum introduced by
the British was at first centred on language studies.[15] Horace
Wilson, a pupil of the Indologist Sir William Jones and a Sanskrit scholar, among others criticised this pedagogical mode on
the premise that "mere language cannot work any material
change". It was his conviction that

we initiate them into our literature particularly at an early age, and get them to adopt feelings and sentiments from our standard writers we make an impression upon them and effect any considerable alteration in their feelings and *notions*. (*Parliamentary Papers* 1852-53, Vol. 32: 266)

The missionaries, in contrast, contended that while European education might doubtless help demolish "heathen" superstition; "moral" instruction was indispensable for a well-rounded schooling of the native. The teaching of the Bible instead of a secular syllabus in their view was a responsibility of the British educators. The teaching of religion to the poor in Britain had traditionally been seen as a telling means of containing social disquiet. Ian Michael, for example, writing on the compilers of anthologies used in British schools in the nineteenth century, comments: "The compilers do not discuss, or seem to recognise, any difference between religious poetry and versified doctrine". He cites the hope harboured by one compiler ('one of Her Majesty's Inspectors of Church Schools')

that the 'children of the peasantry and artisans' would come to understand and 'sympathise with sentiments and principles by which well educated persons are influenced' and 'to understand and sympathise with the views of the superiors'. Because such children 'are frequently at a loss to understand the forms, which persons of cultivated minds are accustomed to use in expressing their thoughts' they are open to persuasion by the 'socialist infidel'. (1987: 221)

The domestic education policy that advocated instruction in Christian principles seemed to be oriented toward control – echoing unwittingly Marx's description of religion as the opium of the masses. The impulse to moralise the poor and the project of education were intimately connected in that hegemony, in Gramsci's sense, which underlay the educational objectives of the Victorian 'experts' (see Johnson 1977; also

Stallybrass and White 1986). An educational curriculum tailored on these lines in the colonies would, the missionaries argued, have the double advantage of expanding the market for trade. "Wherever our principles and our language are introduced", Charles Grant suggested, disregarding the supposed opposition between the spiritual and the material, "our commerce will follow" (1797: 220).

The spectre of native insurgency always provided the backcloth for any policy, especially educational policy for the colony. Missionary thinking consistently stressed "moral improvement" (by which was meant Christian religious education) as the only forestalling device against native insubordination. The fear that the introduction of Christian values itself might provide the stepping stone for Indians to aspire toward self-rule was vehemently rejected by Charles Grant in 1832:

The establishment of Christianity in a country does not necessarily bring after it a free political constitution. The early Christians made no attempts to change forms of Government; ... Christianity seeks moral good, and general happiness. It does not, in the pursuit of these objects erect a peculiar political system; it views politics through the safe medium of morals, and subjects them to the law of universal rectitude. (quoted in Hutchins 1967: 13)

Yielding to such contentions was out of the question for the powers that controlled the East India Company. That the moralising and civilising missions would lead to the institutionalisation of church edification was an anxiety connected to the fear of subaltern insurgency. The avoidance of insurrections, like the one in Vellore in 1806, had become one of the main priorities of the administration.

The abolition of *sati* (or widow sacrifice) in 1829, for instance, served as a moral alibi for intervention and for the legitimisation of the imperialist project. "The colonial ambivalence towards sati", as in other spheres, was "productive for the achievement of the diverse goals of imperialism" (Sunder Rajan 1993: 48; see also Lata Mani 1984).[16]

Viswanathan's pioneering work on the beginnings of English literary studies in India relates the imposition of literature to the Janus-faced momentum of missionary insistence on hegemony in education and the growing disquietude over subaltern restiveness:

Provoked by missionaries on the one hand and fears of native subordination on the other, British administrators discovered an ally in English literature to support them in maintaining control of the natives under the guise of a liberal education. With both secularism and religion appearing as political liabilities, literature appeared to represent a perfect synthesis. (1987: 17)[17]

The policymakers were cautious in including only those texts into the curriculum, which would be conducive to "moral" pedagogy. With this in view, Addison's *Spectator* papers, Adam Smith's *Moral Sentiments*, and some of the works of Bacon, Locke and Shakespeare appeared on the syllabus.[18]

These and other canonised texts were used to serve as an example of English Literature, an exalted mode of intellectual production, in contrast to indigenous texts in Indian languages. 'English' as "an accepted canon of works in a clearly defined national language" (MacCabe 1985: 5) of course never existed until the gradual consolidation in Britain of literature as a body of knowledge. As a repository of objective and universally valid knowledge culled with the tools of rationalism, English literature, it was claimed by these educators, prepared the intellect for the tasks of rationality (like Latin before it) and sagacious argument. The new education policy was intended to produce students who would approach a given subject in a detached, rational manner. Questions set in the examinations demanded analyses but left little room for unfettered conclusions (cf. Hill and Parry 1994).[19] The following fairly regular essay topics display a tortured sort of rationality at

best: "On the Internal Marks of Falsehood in the Hindu Shas-
tras"; "On the Merits of Christianity and the Demerits of
Hinduism"; "The Advantages India Derived in Regard to
Commerce, Security of Property, and the Diffusion of Know-
ledge from its Connexion with England" (*Parliamentary
Papers 1852-53*, Vol 29: 452-53; 491-617).[20]

The educational system not only actively took on the prop-
agation of English as the medium of instruction, it gradually valorised English literary studies. Thus, the Bengal
government's proposal to build up Hindu and Muslim colleges and bolster the publication of Indian classical works was rejected on arrival for approval at the India House in London.
James Mill, whose views wielded immense power and was
critical of the Orientalist glorification of Indian tradition, put
forward the case for western education in India:

> The great end should not have been to Hindu learning or to Moham-
> medan learning, but useful learning .... In professing to establish semin-
> aries for the purpose of teaching mere Hindu or mere Mohammedan lit-
> erature, you bound yourself to teach a great deal of what was frivolous,
> not a little of what was purely mischievous .... (*Parliamentary Papers
> 1831-32*, IX: 488)

Oriental scholarship was devalued and all patronage for it
withdrawn. All that was meant (or desired) to be known had
already congealed in comfortable stereotypical knowledge;
any need for further scholarship was at best redundant. The
Government, in a Resolution dated 7th March 1835, categor-
ically stated that no portion of the fund set aside for educational purposes might be used in printing oriental works (Trevelyan 1838: 14). Thus, extensive plans for the publication of
Arabic and Sanskrit works were immediately suspended as
were medical classes held in Indian languages.

Nationalist Discourse on Education

In a sense, the strategic aims of the colonial education project were more deeply realised than its planners would have hoped for. The British mission of self-representation – of projecting colonialism as an even-handed, upright and moral rule – and the project for the production of a Macaulayan civil society found widespread resonance among the native intelligentsia. In the field of education, nationalist discourse, as Kumar has remarked, "developed an idiom that was homonymous with the idiom used by the colonial rulers" (1992: 152).[21]

At the time of the appointment of the *Committee of Public Instruction* in 1823, native enthusiasm for Anglicised education was exemplified in the person of Rammohun Roy. The latter pleaded for "promoting a more liberal and enlightened system of instruction embracing mathematics, natural philosophy, chemistry and anatomy, with other sciences" in place of the proposed Sanskrit college (1945-58; Part 4: 108). More generally, the Brahmos (of which Roy was one) and Derozians were convinced that the Anglicisation of education would take the country forward by developing "India's productive forces through the introduction of modern science and technology and capitalistic economic organisation" (Chandra 1987-88: 91).

Accepting the colonial presumption that the antiquated system of indigenous education – incoherent and disorganised, at the best of times – had wholly atrophied during the twilight years of Mughal rule, the native intelligentsia argued for a radical overhaul of the traditional system of learning comprising *tals* and *madrassahs* (seats of higher Sanskrit and Arabic learning) together with *pathshalas, maktabs* ('Hindu' and 'Muslim' elementary schools respectively) and *gurukuls* (schools for Vedic instruction).[22]

Many regarded the arrival of the British as a divine blessing which ought to, as Hindi litterateur Bharatendu Harishchandra once famously remarked, awaken the "slothful slum-

ber" of Indians (Kumar 1991: 149-51). In Bengal, Keshab
Chandra Sen went one better. Alien rule in India, he said, "is
not a man's work but a work which God is doing with His own
Hands, using [the] British nation as His instrument" (1938:
90).[23]

Within the parameters of bourgeois-liberal ideology, the
native intelligentsia in colonial India was fascinated by the
prospect of a future fashioned by the liberalism (it was not
before the first quarter of the twentieth century that some
leaned towards Marxism) of Mill, Spencer, Rousseau and
Thomas Paine (see Pannikar 1987: 2117). It was in this context
that Dadabhoy Naoroji once characterised colonial rule as un-
British, meaning thereby that it didn't always fulfil the noble
ideals for which it was institutionalised. Ram Mohan Roy
labelled England as a nation of people:

[not only] blessed with the enjoyment of a civil and political liberty but
[who] also interest themselves in promoting liberty and social happiness, as well as free inquiry into literary and religious subjects among
those nations to which their influence extends. (quoted in Pannikar
1985: 415)

The chief architect in the implementation of educational policy
in India, C.E. Trevelyan, maintained that the finest desire of
the natives was to catapult themselves to the cerebral and
moral rank of the rulers. His inference in 1838 was that "we have
gained everything by our superior knowledge; that it is this
superiority which enabled us to conquer India, and to keep it".

It goes without saying that British educational policy produced individuals who were alienated from their own culture
and the mass of Indian society. This awareness of a denation-
alised middle class is present in periodicals, such as the *Tattvabodhini Patrika* and *The Bengal Spectator*, of that time: "[we]
blindly imitate what others have done" (quoted in Pannikar
1987: 2119). A pundit from South India in 1866, Lingam
Lakshmaji Pantlu Garu, had unlimited faith in English know-

ledge and what it could do for India. "A man that has received
a thorough English education is fit for everything that is good
and laudable" (1866: 20). His only complaint was that the
British "look upon us as beings of an inferior order" which
surely "tend[s] to demoralise us and to estrange us" (35). Ambivalent about these demoralising effects, he attributes them,
like his masters, to India's own past: "We lie; we steal; we
desire; we commit rape … and then early in the morning we
bathe in the Ganges, whose filthy waters wash away our sins"
(28). The English-educated minority drawn from the middle
classes became collaborators or 'native informants' crucial to
the day-to-day functioning of the Empire (Dirks 1993). This
middle class was on the ascendancy particularly after the
revolt or uprising of 1857, which marked the demise of the
indigenous ruling class.

Attempts to produce a sense of inadequacy and a dependency complex in the minds of the colonised were largely effect-
ed through a certain kind of educational discourse[24] (see Walsh
1983). Examinations manifestly designed to teach students to
consider "objectively" such themes as the "Demerits of Hinduism" could lead to a debasement of inherited cultural traditions. K.N. Pannikar, among other historians, observes that
"the colonizer created and propagated several myths about the
character and capacity of the colonised which in course of time
[some of] the colonised themselves began to believe" (1985:
420). Deception, untruthfulness, undependability, and similarly negative characteristics imagined as common Indian attributes became an integral element of the self-image of India (or
of certain classes) in this era. The legacy of that self-representation persists in that "today the English-educated elite readi-
ly ascribes these qualities to the masses" (1985: 420).

A generation after the institution of English as the official
language in India, literary activity in the colonisers' language
emerged. The Indian novel in English began as a colonial venture vaguely aspiring to continue the English tradition. The
literary models of Bankim Chandra Chatterjee's *Rajmohan's*

Wife (1864) and Toru Dutt's *Bianca* (1878) were European and
the authors clearly aspired to be what Michael Madhusadan
Dutt characterised as "gents who fancy that they are swarthy
Macaulays and Carlyles and Thackerays". Dutt himself was
scarcely less complicitous, attempting an epic on the Miltonic
model: "Nothing can be better than Milton ... . I don't think
it impossible to equate Virgil, Kalidas and Tasso. Though glorious, still they are mortal poets. Milton is divine" (cited in
Gupta 1963: 146).[25]

There was, of course, considerable variation among nineteenth century intellectuals in their opinions about European
culture. It ranged from the cultural chauvinism of Pandit Sasadhar Tarkachudamani (famous for 'certifying' the 'scientific'
basis of Hinduism) and Haji Muhammad Hashim to the an-
glophilia of the Derozians. Ambivalence towards tradition and
modernity can be seen in Rammohun Roy's mix of reform
and compromises with orthodoxy (see Sarkar 1985) and the
assertive Hinduism of Bankimchandra who drew from such
disciplines as "comparative philology, sociology, the study of
myths, Christian higher criticism and the methodology of 'scientific history'" (Raychaudhuri 1988: 148). Bhudev Mukho-
padhyaya and Vivekananda, for instance, were both products
of western education but preoccupied with the projection of a
Hindu way of life and whose "perceptions of Europe became
part of the region's [Bengal's] cultural heritage and even influenced popular stereotypes" (Raychaudhuri 1988: xiii).

But Bankim, especially, is too complex a figure to sum up and
place in such a neat way. Recent studies by Chatterjee (1986),
Kaviraj (1995), and others suggest the ambivalence in his attitudes.[26] Bankim typifies, writes Chatterjee, the unresolved contradiction in nationalist thought which, on the one hand, emphasises the modern and thus seeks tutelage and "collaboration"
with the West, and yet, on the other hand, sets itself ideologically to strongly espouse what is distinctly national (1986: 80-81).
Bankim's is a case which "certainly cannot be dismissed easily as
either revivalist or 'native informant'" (Loomba 1991: 181).

In a shorthand way, this signals the beginning of a phase where the native intellectual's assimilated identity stands ruptured, with the pre-colonial past re-emerging in the lived and living experiences of the colonised.[27] As Ahmad notes:

Rare would be a text of our canonical nationalism (witness, for example, the agnostic, socialist Mr Nehru's *Discovery of India*) which did not assume that 'spirituality' was the special vocation of the Indian in World history. Positivist kinds of secularism and modernism which grew during the same period often found it difficult to withstand these pressures for identifying Indian cultural nationalism with metaphysics and revivalist tendencies. (1992: 276)

One example of this kind of stimulus was Rabindranath Tagore's work which, in terms of mimeticist poetics, contained, on the one hand, mystical elements, and, on the other, the tensions between modernity and an abiding nostalgia for the feudal order. Tagore indeed was later to testify to the dominance of English literary culture in Indian education:

Our literary gods then were Shakespeare, Milton and Byron … .The frenzy of Romeo's and Juliet's love, the fury of King Lear's impotent lamentation, the all-consuming fire of Othello's jealousy, these were the things that roused us to enthusiastic admiration. (1921: 181-82)

Tagore was, of course, the archetypal *bhadralok*[28] with an ambivalence about his own identity: "when in the village I become an Indian. The moment I go to Calcutta I become a European. Who knows which is my true self?" (quoted in Moorhouse 1983: 203).

Bhadraloks like Tagore and even Ram Mohan Roy can be placed in a Eurocentric-Orientalist bind aspiring to evolve an indigenous modern culture but, in the words of an historian who has studied the cultural formation in nineteenth century Bengal, also inherit[ing] from the two schools their common socially exclusive attitude of total indifference to certain socio-economic and historical factors – the unequal access among the indigenous population to western education, which was bound to make 'European thoughts and literary forms' a jealously guarded preserve of the privileged few; the hierarchical features of the indigenous traditional culture separating courtly culture from folk culture, the esoteric from the popular in the religious and ideological movements from the past; the occupational division of labour in nineteenth century Calcutta which gave birth to two separate streams of culture. (Bannerjee 1989: 7)

Nearly fifty years of political independence has not yielded a clear sense of cultural self-sufficiency. The ambivalence can be seen in government publications on education and culture. Departments of literature, for instance, are still called English departments (like their reification in the U.S.A.) and they continue to teach British literature almost exclusively. One reason for this, it seems, is that the Indian National Congress never attempted a thoroughgoing social revolution, but almost entirely adopted the political and bureaucratic structures established by the British Raj. Nationalism as an oppositional discourse and the construction of nationalist intellectuals occurred primarily through the repressive and discursive state apparatuses of the empire. An analysis of the social composition of the nationalist movement would probably reveal the degree to which nationalist intellectuals are formed within the colonial state. "Official nationalisms", writes Anderson

were historically 'impossible' until after the appearance of popular linguistic-nationalisms, for at bottom, they were *responses* by power-groups – primarily, but not exclusively, dynastic and aristocratic – threatened with exclusion from, or marginalization in, popular imagined communities … . Such official nationalisms were conservative, not to say reactionary, *policies*, adapted from the model of the largely spontaneous popular nationalisms that preceded them. Nor were they ultimately confined to Europe and the Levant. In the name of imperialism, very similar policies were pursued by the same sorts of groups in the vast Asian and African territories subjected in the course of the nineteenth century. (1983: 109-10)

Nationalism in the post-colonial state can still be seen as dependent on imperial forms, as a continuation of the anti-colonial nationalism of the colonial era (Chatterjee 1986).[29]

The success of the Raj ideology is apparent not only in departments of English and in the production of fictions that are specifically targeted for a 'western' readership,[30] but is even more powerfully evident in intellectual histories of colonial India. Only in the last two decades or so have historians challenged the notion that European thought and knowledge, specifically English education, were the catalysts that brought about a socio-cultural regeneration in India.[31] Following the colonial ideologues, Indians have generally seen Britain's intervention in India as fundamentally a civilising mission:

A new ideology burst forth upon the static life, moulded for centuries by fixed sets of religious ideas and conventions. It gave birth to a critical attitude towards religion and a spirit of inquiry into the origin of state and society with a view to determining their proper scope and function. (Mazumdar 1965: 89)

Jadunath Sarkar, for example, saw the period between Robert Clive and Hastings as "the land recover[ing] from the blight of mediaeval theocratic rule" (1973: 497-98), and modernity as succeeding the dark 'Muslim period' of James Mill's *History* and dispelling the static oriental despotism of Montesquieu. Scholars, both Indian and western, have continued to assume rather simplistically that western education and institutions provided the push needed to change the moribund Indian society of the nineteenth century. "The stimulating forces", writes Farquhar, "are almost exclusively Western, viz., the British Government, English education and literature, Christianity, oriental research, European science and philosophy, and the material elements of Western civilisation" (1967: 433).

Charles Heimsath (1969) attributes not only ideas but even methods of organisation adopted by Indians to western inspiration. Nirad Chaudhuri, the most notorious of anglophiles, could conclude amidst the chaos of Indian independence: "'Civis Britannicus Sum', because all that was good and living within was made, shaped, and quickened by the same British rule [as the England of Shakespeare, Milton, etc.]" (1951: v).

Nehru, the nationalist historian, although keen about modernity and rationalism saw the period that Sarkar above enthuses over as 'outright plunder' and 'pure loot', and as leading to the famine of 1770 which wiped away a third of the population of Bihar and Bengal (1974: 297).[32] Nehru's critical modernist attempt to articulate the space between the western sign and its colonial signification is a vital link between the concerns of this chapter and the last.

Notes

1   The reference is from Marx's famous essay of 1853, 'The British Rule in India': "England, it is true, in causing a social revolution in Hindustan was actuated only by the vilest interests, and was stupid in her manner of enforcing them. But that is not the question. The question is, can mankind fulfil its destiny without a fundamental revolution in the social state of truth? If not, whatever may have been the crimes of England she was the unconscious tool of History in bringing about that revolution" (Marx & Engels 1959: 41).

2   The British colonial state also strove to find legitimacy in a moralisation of the 'rule of law'. Thus, a legal member of the viceroy Lord Mayo's Council wrote: "The establishment of a system of law which regulates the most important parts of the daily life of the people constitutes in itself a moral conquest more striking, more durable, and more solid, than the physical conquest which rendered it possible" (quoted in Metcalf 1994: 39).

3 Burke was Hastings' arch-rival. As Musselwhite notes, "… much of what was at stake in the Hastings trial derived from [the] struggle between the Tory-Whigism [landed and aristocratic interests] represented by Burke and the emerging monied interest represented by Hastings" (1986: 84).

4 These ideas, it is argued, came from the Physiocrats in France. See Ranajit Guha's *A Rule of Property for Bengal: The Idea of Permanent Settlement* (1982).

5 See also Cornwallis' Minute dated 18 September 1789. For full reference see next note.

6 Citing from Cornwallis' Minute dated 18 September 1789 (in G. Forrest (ed.), *Selections from the State papers of the Governors-General of India. Lord Cornwallis* (London, 1914), ii, 79) C. A. Bayly writes: "dispensing with 'native agency' and its replacement by a disciplined cadre of European collectors of revenue and judges would hasten the demise of what Cornwallis saw as 'Asiatic tyranny' and the corruption of public office" (1988: 65-66).

7 Bayly points out that "Cornwallis argued that the Company's trade itself was in danger 'because agriculture must flourish before its [Bengal's] commerce can become extensive'. The way to create a flourishing agriculture was to stabilise a hereditary landed aristocracy" (65).

8 He justified British Imperialism, in 'Memorandum on Bengal', on the grounds that it was "founded upon the policy usually adopted by modern and ancient nations in regard to conquered territories" (quoted in Owen 1800: 503). The Wellesley generation infused the administration "with a new single-mindedness which emphasized the power and dignity of the state, the morality of conquest and British racial superiority" (Bayly 1988: 81).

9 The Fort William College was meant to "extricate the young public servants from the 'habitual indolence, dissipation and licentious indulgence' which were the 'natural consequence' of living in close proximity to the 'peculiar' depravity of the people of India'" (Bayly 1988: 83, citing from *Minute in Council at Fort William, 18 August 1800, Asiatic Annual Register,* 1802: 129).

10 The 1854 despatch of Sir Charles Wood sets out these objectives

clearly. There is a stress on the generation of a class of Indians who, in following their European superiors, would spawn a demand for British goods, as well as an emphasis on the dissemination of western culture. This would result in teaching the natives the benefits of "the employment of labour and capital" for the development of the country, and "secure to us a large and more certain supply of many articles necessary for our manufactures ... as well as an almost inexhaustible demand for the product of British labour" (*Parliamentary Papers 1854*).

11 The conflict between Parliament and the East India Company had partly to do with the rise of the free trade era and subsequent demands for de-monopolising the Company's trade in India (see Bowen 1991). Perhaps, more importantly, Parliament was becoming increasingly threatened by the political power the Company wielded. Pitt's India Bill of 1784 specifically rejected the unconditional subordination of the Company to the Crown. A specious reason to intervene in the affairs of the Company was provided by the criticisms of the excesses committed by the English Nabobs or gentleman-capitalists who had amassed wealth in India (Spear 1963). Disguised as concern for the well-being of the natives, Parliament's expanded involvement by the end of the eighteenth century marked the weakening of the Company and its subsequent demise.

12 The theme of the 'Indian character', as one might expect, was a favourite one. I will restrict myself to just one citation from Lord Wellesley on the Indian people: "vulgar, ignorant, rude, familiar and stupid" (quoted in Spear 1963: 145). Qualities such as these in Indian character could be traced to, it was argued, ancient Indian literature. This literature instructed that "revenge is to be cherished, and truth is not to be rewarded as a virtue, or falsehood as a crime" (*Parliamentary Papers 32*: 29).

13 Javed Majeed (1992), among others, has noted the British reliance on local networks of power.

14 "Macaulay had said little that was new", Stokes writes, "everywhere his speech rings with ideas which the older Charles Grant and Wilberforce had uttered forty years before" (1959: 54).

15 That the learning of classical languages inculcates mental discipline

was widely accepted at the time in England. J.W. Hales in 1867 (much later than when the case was being made for India) was one of the first to advocate the institutional study of English grammar, "that the linguistic studies of all our schools should begin with English, should then proceed with the dead languages in the case of the boys who are likely to have leisure to study them to any profit, and in other cases should proceed with English and living languages" (quoted in Farrar 1867: 301). In *The Report of the Royal Commission known as the Schools Inquiry Commission of 1868 (The Taunton Report)* there also is a noticeable shift in opinion among educationists speaking in favour of English language and literature teaching. Thus Earl Harrowby: "I do believe it will be of the most infinite moral advantage to our nation if our youth of every class were accustomed to read our best books in literature from their earliest days, proportional of course to their age and their condition in various ways; but if they were accustomed to read the most interesting and profitable books in English literature, I believe the moral as well as intellectual effect would be enormous" (5: 534). That the matter was not simply one of English versus the classics, is borne out by his argument for social control: "I take the problem as of an ordinary boy from ordinary classes going into an ordinary career in life, and over whom you have control only till the age of 13, 14 or 15. Well then, I say, what is the best use to make over those years during which you have control over him?" (5: 534). I am grateful to David Johnson for pointing out this source to me. For the South African dimension of the argument, see his excellent essay, 'Aspects of a Liberal Education: Late nineteenth century Attitudes to Race, from Cambridge to Cape Colony', *History Workshop Journal 36*, 1993. See J. Stuart Maclure, *Educational Documents. England and Wales 1816-1963*, (1965) pp.89-97 for a summary of *The Taunton Report*.

16 Spivak too has shown this about colonial intervention with the case of the Rani of Sirmur when the latter decides to commit suicide. The dissuading officials were not impelled by any higher motives but simply by the cognition that in the continuation of the Rani's rule lay "the commercial/territorial interests of the East India Com-

pany" (Spivak 1987: 263). But for Spivak, since there is no "real
Rani" to be found and since the subaltern "cannot speak", she, in
her role as postcolonial critic, undertakes to "give the subaltern a
voice in history" (Parry 1987: 35).

17 Examinations had already been taking place in India much before
they were instituted in England (Viswanathan 1989: 23-44). *The
Taunton Report* (1867) did not result immediately in legislating the
introduction of English literature in England. Nevertheless, literature had entered the curriculum by the 1870s. With the establishment of public examinations, inducement to include English literature in secondary schools had grown. The Royal Charter was issued
only in 1849 and in 1859 English language and literature became a
subject in its own right at London University for matriculating as
well as graduating students. The Indian Civil Service examiner
W.G. Dasent in *The Taunton Report* makes a case for restricting the
knowledge of English literature to the upper classes and making it
inaccessible to the class "just above the National schools, which includes the superior artizan, the foreman of works, and the lower
shopkeeper" and that they should be limited to "the rudiments of
English" (1868: 528). *The Cross Report* (1888) made much the same
case: "Care must be taken lest in attempting to raise too much the
standard of education the country might defeat the object for which
education was given, namely, the manual labour in which so many
children must be occupied afterwards" (quoted in Shayer 1972: 94)

18 The term 'literature' in the nineteenth century embraced scientific
reports, moral essays, political tracts, etc., within its fold. Raymond
Williams in *Keywords* (1976) has mapped out the different trajec-
tories in its movement: "All works within the orbit of polite learning came to be described as literature and all such interests and
practices as literary. Thus Hazlitt, in *Of Persons One would Wish to
Have Seen (Winterslow, II)*, reports: 'Ayrton said, "I suppose the
two first persons you would choose to see would be the two greatest names in English literature, Sir Isaac Newton and Mr Locke" '
(c. 1825)". He goes on to say that "English Literature seems to have
followed the notion of "a *Nationallitteratur* developed in Germany
from the 1770s" and "[t]he sense of 'a nation' having 'a literature'

is a crucial social and cultural, probably also political, development" (Williams 1976: 185).

19 Clifford Hill and Kate Parry (1994) have shown that such an approach to pedagogy can hardly be responsive to the needs of non-native (i.e. non-native to English) learners.

20 These questions are contained in two of the many appendices to the *Parliamentary Papers 1852-1853*: (i) Statement of the Progress and Success of the General Assembly Institution at Calcutta and (ii) General Report on Public Instruction in the Lower Provinces of the Bengal Presidency for 1843-1844. The vernacular educated were also influenced (see Pannikar 1985: 414-19).

21 The two figures who stand out of this homonymy are Tagore and Gandhi. Both offered, in their own ways, a more humanistic and indigenous line and stood against the general nationalist discourse which was responding in little more than a knee-jerk sort of manner to the colonial project. Although his experiments in pedagogy reflected an inclination towards modernism, Tagore's critique of colonial education was largely an indictment on the lack of a common education system for all. Because it was narrowly focussed, the system produced a class of men cut off from their own context. The Indian students, deprived of the opportunity to learn through the medium of their 'natural' language "never see in the right perspective the environment and the process of growth of those thoughts which they are compelled to learn" (Tagore 1961: 208) His experiment which established Shantiniketan was inspired, among other things, by his fond remembrance of a reading of Defoe's *Robinson Crusoe*. He found it to be "one of the best books for boys ever written". It was "particularly Indian" in the nature of its disposition towards "the expansion of consciousness". Its portrayal of "harmony with nature attained through intelligent dealings" signified a Rousseauistic essence in the West's adventurous but rationalist spirit (Tagore 1961: 293).

Gandhi's proposal for Basic Education was as radical as it was sweeping in the context of his ideas for the socio-economic reconstruction of India. His was a total rejection of English education as it was a component of his wider critique of western civilisation.

Gandhi is not within, to use Chatterjee's phrase, "the thematic of nationalism", the "conceptual framework or the modes of reasoning and influence adopted by the nationalists of his day". He "quite emphatically rejects their rationalism, scientism and historicism" (1986: 93). What he was striving for was an alternative model of development that would not only suit the conditions and needs of India but also challenge the firmly established notion and practice (although not yet a discursive mode in the postcolonial sense) of development. His proposal in the late 1930s for a "basic national education" was a plan not rooted in nationalism but a response to what he saw as the merciless mechanisation of living. Industrialisation, he asserted, led to the ills of colonialism, poverty and illiteracy (See Gandhi 1938).

22 Archival evidence in the form of reports submitted by Collectors to Governors and their minutes from 1826 suggest that local institutions of learning were widespread in the eighteenth century and their composition was not always caste and sex based (see Dharmpal 1983). The Collector of Bellary, A.D. Campbell's Report of 17 August 1823, for instance, stands against the general view of writers who tended to easily denigrate the pre-existing system of indigenous education without taking into account the violence of colonialism: "I am sorry to state, that this is ascribable to the gradual but general impoverishment of the country. The means of the manufacturing classes have been of late years greatly diminished by the introduction of our European manufactures in lieu of the Indian cotton fabrics ... the transfer of the capital of the country from the native governments and their officers who liberally expended it in India, to Europeans ... has likewise tended to this effect ... . Thus greater part of the middling (sic.) and lower classes of the people are now unable to defray the expenses incident upon the education of their off-spring ... . Of the 553 institutions for education now existing in this District, I am ashamed to say that not one now derives any support from the State ... . Considerable alienation of revenue which formerly did honour to the State, by upholding and encouraging learning, have deteriorated under our rule in to the means of supporting ignorance" (quoted in Basu 1952: 181-83).

23 This is reminiscent of what Fanon calls the assimilative phase, the first phase, when the native intellectual responds to the colonial presence in a certain way which gives proof "that he has assimilated the culture of the occupying power. His writings correspond point by point with those of his opposite numbers in the mother country. His inspiration is European and we can easily link up these works with definite trends in the literature of the mother country. This is the period of unqualified assimilation" (1967: 178-79).

24 Viswanathan (1989), for instance, cites the case of Nobinchunder Dass, a student of Hooghly College, Calcutta, who internalised, like Lingam Garu cited above, all the aims of British education to the extent that he can refer to his fellow Indians as 'the natives'.

25 Dutt exemplifies, in Fanon's words, the "universal standpoint": "This is because the native intellectual has thrown himself greatly upon Western culture. Like adopted children who only stop investigating the new family framework at the moment when a minimum nucleus of security crystallizes in their psyche, the native intellectual will try to make European culture his own. He will not be content to get to know Rabelais and Diderot, Shakespeare and Edgar Allan Poe; he will bind them to his intelligence as tightly as possible" (1967: 176).

In *Black Skin, White Masks* Fanon examines further the psychic dimension of colonisation and how the western archetypes enter the unconscious of the colonised: "The *anima* of the Antillean Negro is almost always a white woman. In the same way, the *animus* of the Antilleans is always a white man. That is because in the works of Anatole France, Balzac, Bazin, or any of the rest of "our" novelists, there is never a word about an ethereal yet ever present black woman or about a dark Apollo with sparkling eyes … . But I too am guilty, here I am talking about Apollo! There is no help for it: I am a white man. For unconsciously I distrust what is black in me, that is, the whole of my being" (1986: 191).

26 "Imprisoned within the rationalist framework of his theoretical discourse and powerless to reject its dominating implications, Bankim lived out his dreams of liberation in his later novels. In form, *Anandmath* (1882), *Devi Chaudhurani* (1884) and *Sitaram* (1887)

are historical romances, but they are suffused with a utopianism
which, by the power of the particular religious semiotic in which it
was expressed, had a deep emotional influence on the new intelligentsia" (Chatterjee 1986: 79).

27 In Fanon's terms this would refer to the second phase of colonialism, a phase in which "we spew ourselves up" (1967: 179).

28 The term *bhadralok* literally refers to 'respectable folk' as opposed
to *chhotolok*, which means 'lowly folk' (see Sinha and Bhattacharya
1969). As an elite group, it signifies a kind of ethos that draws from
eastern (i.e., pre-British Hindu culture) as well as western intellec-
tualism (see Shils 1961).

29 To come back to Fanon. The problem with his three-phase genealo-
gy is that it imposes a reading of Indian nationalism as a diachron-
ic evolution, as an apprenticeship for the elites negotiating (with an
aborted third phase displacing the subaltern) to carry on the complex machinery of colonialism.

30 Sarojini Naidu had thus turned to writing about the bulbul and the
sitar at the advice of Edmund Gosse. Her poem 'In the Bazaars of
Hyderabad' is a perfect recreation of an orientalized market. The
fictions of Kamala Markandaya and Manohar Malgonkar evoke the
British sense of 'honour and justice' and the splendorous nostalgia
of the Raj.

31 Partha Mitter's *Much Maligned Monsters: A History of European
Reactions to India* (1977) was one of the first books to challenge the
myth of exclusive European sagacity and, in particular, Europe's
failure to appreciate the arts of India.

32 In his essay, 'On National Culture', Fanon analyses the dialectical
process by which a bourgeois anti-colonial nationalism may be displaced by a popular nationalism in the post-independence state
which is not the underling of a fetishized 'national culture'. This of
course can be construed as furnishing the basis of a critique of the
subaltern school of historiography which, to simplify somewhat,
deprecates the anti-modernist and Manichean inclination of nationalism and has to accept British imperialism as a fundamentally
modernising impulse (1967: 166-99).

CHAPTER THREE

'The State of Culture'
National Imaginings

> *spread much more Knowledge and Civility, yea, Religion,*
> *through all parts of the Land, by communicating the natural*
> *heat of Government and Culture more distributively to all ex-*
> *treme parts, which now lie num and neglected*
>
> Milton quoted in Williams 1976: 78

> *Culture is not a thing but has to be dressed up as one in social*
> *scientific discourse in order to be defined.*
>
> Street 1993: 25

The battle over truth in its politico-economic role-playing dimension is crucial in understanding the significance of official discourse, especially in the realm of education and culture. Complicitous with social science,[1] state discourse seeks to depict the world in 'real' or factual terms from which certain valorised practices are seen to follow as 'natural' consequences. This seamless coupling puts forward a vision of society that resonates with national feeling. Thus come into being, as Barthes (1973) has demonstrated, modern social mythologies.

The claim to truth with regard to culture masks significant continuities in colonial and postcolonial official discourses. Their shared epistemic assumptions, for instance, constitute a veritable silence on structural social inequalities and marginalised identities. Articulated in a deceptively self-evident and 'neutral' value framework, this silence first disavows real divisions in the body politic and then, in a contradictory reversal, celebrates them as natural and inevitable. Discourse, then, is a privileged language that "approaches us from without; it is distanced, taboo, and permits no play with its framing context" (Bakhtin 1984: 424).

By favouring discourse over 'policy' or 'public policy', I locate the problem of culture in a discursive space, a certain way of seeing and doing things, rather than merely argue for or against the nature of policy as such. State or public policy, is but a part, however significant, of official discourse. In that sense it is a 'place' of the powerful where the 'space' for intervention by the powerless is ruled out (see de Certeau 1984).[2]

Policy is the specification of a course or pattern of purposive action in the face of a problem or issue and is aimed towards the achievement of certain goals. These goals, in a democracy, are defined by the government. The political and intellectual bases of a policy prescription are often laid down in reports submitted by state-sponsored commissions of inquiry. The public, advisory, and *ad hoc* nature of these commissions serves to establish their claims to disinterestedness. Ideally, they operate as a consultative space where state policy pertaining to certain problems, projects, etc., is negotiated. (Not so ideally, they can be used to delay action by the government. The recommendations contained in reports are quite regularly ignored.) The involvement of the civil service secretariats in the production of these reports anoints them with an official halo, the involvement of relevant 'experts' gives them an air of intellectual legitimacy, even superiority.[3]

The recently released report of the "High Powered Review Committee" (*sic*) under the chairmanship of P. N. Haksar, set up following a resolution of the Government of India (Department of Culture, Ministry of Human Resource Development, 1988), is a typical example of the how the issue of culture is brought into the domain of official discourse.

The report purports to present an exhaustive and represen-

tative overview of the state of culture in the country by reviewing the workings of the Sangeet Natak, Lalit Kala and Sahitya Akademis, together with their affiliates and subsidiaries
and the National School of Drama. "We have been able to secure", the report claims, "an integral view of the cultural scene
in our country" (1990: 4). The report's ambitious scope,
echoed in the self-importance of its title, involved scrutinising
the "records of institutions, including the agenda and proceedings of their policy-making, executive and academic bodies
and internal committees". Apart from "benefiting" from the
insights of the earlier Review Committees chaired by Dr. H.J.
Bhabha (1964), and Justice G.D. Khosla (1970-72), it also con-
tacted "a nation-wide cross-section of people who are active in
various ways in the fields of the performing and visual arts,
language and literature, education and cultural administration", and aimed to give them an opportunity to "express their
views as individuals or as institutional representatives, or in
both capacities" (3).

In analysing the document's confrontation with the unsat-
isfactory 'state of culture', the discussion that follows will consider the text itself as an aspect of ideological state practice. By
locating it within the state apparatus, the analysis will implicitly identify the discursive regularities it shares with other
official discourses. But before I explore the political uses that
the concept of culture has been put to, it is important to point
out a few things.

Culture is inextricable from norms and mores, and any
proper understanding of the concept – which would not put
too improbable a gloss on it – has to acknowledge this reality.
Further, key normative concepts – like 'justice', 'freedom', 'the
good', etc., – which form the bedrock of any culture are, as W.
B. Gallie has famously reminded us, "essentially contested"
(1955-56: 169). In other words, "there are always good reasons
for disputing the propriety" (Gray 1977: 338) of any of the
uses of such concepts. It follows that the meaning of key cultural concepts remains fluid and cannot be rationally fixed,

other than by way of a 'coercive' consensus imposed from
above by the state. This also means that culture is not a static,
reified, essentialist entity (Asad 1979) but a political process.
Hence the salience of "what culture does" over "what culture
is" (Thornton quoted in Street 1993: 25).

THE COLONIAL CONTEXT

Yet, it is culture conceived of as a possession, diffused and dis-
seminated from a centre of power and privilege that underlies
Mathew Arnold's "traditional" understanding of its necessary
function in society. The "great men of culture", he argues are:

> those who have had a passion for diffusing, for making prevail, for car-
> rying from one end of society to the other, the best knowledge, the best
> ideas of their time; who have laboured to divest knowledge of all that
> was harsh, uncouth, difficult, abstract, professional, exclusive; to hu-
> manise it, to make it efficient outside the clique of the cultivated and
> learned, yet still remaining the best knowledge and thought of the time
> and a true source, therefore, of sweetness and light. (1969: 70)

The hegemony of a certain coterie of ideas over other competing ideologies, then, is what constitutes culture in this definition. Notions of cultural transformation, assimilation and
hybridisation are thus given short shrift. Not surprisingly,
Arnold locates the bases of this hegemonic process in the
state:

> a firm and settled course of public order, is requisite if man is to bring
> to maturity anything precious and lasting now, or to found anything
> precious and lasting for the future. Thus in our eyes, the very frame-
> work and exterior order of the State, whoever may administer the State,
> is sacred; and culture is the most resolute enemy of anarchy, because of
> the great hopes and designs for the State which culture teaches us to
> nourish. (204)

But how could a 'settled course of public order' ever give sub-alterns and underclass 'publics', who must struggle to survive, a right to culture? Arnold does not deign to answer the question. For him, any hint of cultural difference, much less pluralism, is an invitation to anarchy. The state must do all it can to suppress difference. In Foucault's terms, culture then becomes a systematic process of exclusion: an inside/outside field so the other can be marginalised or silenced. The non-equation of the valorised 'it' with the differentiated 'other', as many cultural theorists have pointed out, comes to take the aggrandised form of 'nation'. Such ethnocentrism allied to power is instanced in the Anglicist Macaulay's oft-quoted Minute of 1835, which can be seen to have repercussions on the Indian subcontinent far beyond any immediate questions of policy or administration:

I am quite willing to take the oriental learning at the valuation of the Orientalists themselves. I have never found one among them who could deny that a single shelf of a good European library was worth the whole native literature of India and Arabia. The intrinsic superiority of the Western literature is indeed fully admitted by those members of the committee who support the oriental plan of education ... It is, I believe, no exaggeration to say that all the historical information which has been collected in the Sanskrit language is less valuable than what may be found in the paltry abridgements used at preparatory schools in England. In every branch of physical or moral philosophy, the relative position of the two nations is nearly the same. (quoted in Kopf 1980: 504)

Macaulay, as I argued in the preceding chapter, of course was only one among many other pioneers, like Charles Grant and C.E. Trevelyan, who propounded the idea of introducing English education in India as an instrument for maintaining British rule (See Viswanathan 1989). "Macaulay had said little that was new", Eric Stokes relates, "everywhere his speech rings with ideas which the elder Charles Grant and Wilberforce had uttered forty years before. And the instrument which he looked to for gaining this conquest over the mind of India was no different" (1959: 45).

The powerful systematisation of such discourse was significantly at work in the widely influential liberal philosophy of J.S. Mill:

Both nations [India and China] are to nearly an equal degree tainted with the vices of insincerity, dissembling, treacherous, mendacious to an excess which surpasses even the unusual measure of uncultivated society. (quoted in Kopf 1980: 504)

That India, as a civilisation not advanced enough to regulate its affairs rationally, could be governed by England only despotically, is made clear in Mill's treatise *On Liberty* and *Representative Government*. Edward Said points to the connection between utilitarian philosophy and British colonial rule in the subcontinent:

What is striking in Stokes' *The English Utilitarians and India* is how a small body of thinkers – among them Bentham, of course, and both Mills – were able to argue and implement a philosophic doctrine for India's governance, a doctrine in some respects bearing an unmistakable resemblance to Arnold's and Macaulay's views of European culture to all others. (1983: 13)

Such a discourse evidently cannot be taken to be constituted unambiguously.[4] The ambivalence of colonial authority, as Bhabha has contended, displays a problematic relation between empire and nation:

it puts under erasure, not "on trial", the very discourse of civility within which representative government claims its liberty and empire its ethics. (1985: 74)

In his reflections on the cultural impact of European imperialism, Mill prefigured the 'periodization' of modernity:

Before men begin to think much and long on the peculiarities of their own times, they must have begun to think that those times are, or are destined to be, distinguished in a very remarkable manner from the times which preceded them. Mankind is then divided, into those who are still what they were, and those who have changed: into men of the present age, and men of the past. To the former, the spirit of the age is a subject of exultation; to the latter, of terror; to both, of eager and anxious interest. (1962: 3)

Alongside the division of the world into core and periphery, as we might retrospectively describe it, nations can either belong to "the present age" or "the past"; further, the time scale of the centre (or men of the present age) is the universal norm. Modernity is thus constructed as a literal time concept, chronologically marking off calendar time rather than being conceived of as a discursive socio-political grid whose scales are culturally fused with the chronos of the metropolis.

The liberal humanist tradition – whether it appears as Anglicist, Orientalist, or even multiculturalist – is enabled, through such a framework, to argue for the accommodation of diversity within an overarching unity. Diversity – the official ideology of liberal society – then promises the bountiful multiplicity of various conceptions of the good or of the ends of life.[5] But this is a broken promise; as Bhabha says, "[w]estern connoisseurship is the capacity to understand and locate cultures in a universal time-frame that acknowledges their various historical and social contexts only eventually to transcend them and render them transparent" (1990c: 208).

Recall T.S. Eliot's *Notes Towards the Definition of Culture* (1948) – whose influence extends to Indian departments of English – particularly for its notions of 'partial' or 'regional' cultures. In opposition to the idealised view of culture found in Arnold, Eliot debunks the idea of a pure culture: "We are therefore pressed to maintain the ideal of a world culture, while admitting it is something we cannot imagine. We can only conceive it as the logical term of the relations between cultures" (62). He then goes on to attack the idea of local cultures as self-contained and wonders about migratory effects (in the context of settler colonies) on culture: "The people have taken with them only a part of the total culture ... .The culture which develops on the new soil must therefore be bafflingly alike and different from the parent culture ..." (64). Eliot's sense of cultural difference does not push him to develop the idea of 'part' (or, in Bhabha's terms, 'in-between') cultures. Instead, he attempts to pull together three senses of "culture" contingent on whether they are related to an individual, a class or group, or to a whole society. The old totalizing anthropological definition is, on the other hand, attached to "tribes": "if we are considering highly developed societies, and especially our own contemporary society, we have to consider the relationship of the three senses. At this point anthropology passes over into sociology" (20). In other words, the idea of homogeneity can be brought to bear on "tribes" but not on any complex formation. Higher cultures are distinguished by "differentiation of function, so that you can speak of the less cultured and the more cultured strata of society" (124). The function of education is to perpetuate the higher culture: "Education should help to preserve the class and to select the 'elite'" (163). That is to say, Eliot is striving to fuse the sociological use of 'a culture' with an elitist notion of culture.

POSTCOLONIAL[6] RESPONSES

When Mill says that a "man's desires and impulses ... are the expression of his own nature, as it has been developed and modified by his own culture" (1947: 60), he uses the word 'culture' in an ambiguous sense suspended at the point of transition between the older meaning of "the growth and tending of human faculties" (Williams 1977: 1) and the (nascent) modernist ethnographic sense.

An organic, totalising conception of culture – culture understood as the unique expression, in the realm of belief systems, ideas and aesthetic artefacts, of a community and the source of its continuing identity – deriving from the dominant mode of cultural anthropology at the time, was also adopted by some nationalist movements for whom the assertion of indigenous culture against the colonial was an important political strategy. Ironically, but not coincidentally, an overlap can be discerned between western anthropological conceptualisations of cultural 'others' and nationalist self-perceptions.[7]

The concept of a pre-existing cultural community, for instance, originally articulated in nineteenth century colonial anthropological literature, has continued into the post-Independence period in India, and has spawned a pervasive mode of political thinking (Dumont 1970; Dewey 1972). Another, more sophisticated, version of cultural nationalism, one which dissociates the coincidence of cultural boundaries with spatial ones in general, resurrects the idea of openness as the distinguishing mark of Hindu culture. Closure and dogmatism are then attributed to the infiltration of 'foreign' elements resulting from Mughal and British rule. The ability to assimilate components from outside, asserts Ashish Nandy, is the essence of Indian culture:

it is in the nature of traditional India to maintain a certain openness of cultural boundaries, a permeability which allows new influences to flow in and be integrated as a new set of age-old traditions … and for some cultural elements to flow out … These two processes of inflow and outflow determine, at a given point, Indian culture rather than a rigidly defined set of practices or products surviving from society's past. (Nandy 1987: 153)[8]

This is echoed time and again in official positions on the nature of 'Indian culture' (e.g., in the various Annual Reports brought out by the Department of Culture), albeit without the implicit critique of modernity that we find in Nandy and others. Thus, the Draft document of the National Culture Policy 1992:

Culture is a central instrument of discovering, integrating and asserting the national identity of India, which is truly and inevitably pluralistic. Our culture, which being Indocentric, has always been open to global influences and interaction. While resisting any colonisation of mind, the policy believes, our culture should remain in constant dialogue with the world at large in the realm of ideas, perceptions, media and expressions. (4)

The attack on modernity in its different forms (but mostly in its manifestation as capitalist imperialism) has led to the characterisation of pre-modern Hindu civilisation as that which is not just most authentically Indian but bereft of many of the ills which afflict contemporary society. In other words, a certain nostalgia, however sophisticated, for the "glorious past" is built into readings of this kind. Sudipto Kaviraj, for instance, argues that the relatively "decentralised" and "non-conflictual" quality of Indian society is a function of a past ordering of power in the form of a "circle of circles of caste and regional communities with the state sitting at the centre" (1990). The more rigid and centralised ordering of power brought in by the British is then held responsible for the conflicts and divisions in contemporary India (Pandey 1990).

Similarly, with regard to the problem of communalism, it has been argued that it was the process of enumeration of religious communities, conducted by the colonial state, which gave fluid religious communities a transcendental sense of community. The introduction by the British of new political institutions based on the notion of denominational representation helped to further politicise these communities, thus giving rise, over time, to communalism or politicised religious communities (Thapar 1989; Appadurai 1993). This in turn led to the demand, in post-independence India, for western style secularism according to which the state was to be separated from civil society.[9] Attributing the increase of communal violence to this colonial history, social and political theorists like Kaviraj have invoked a benign past with its overlapping and 'fuzzy' identities and notions of tolerance within a shared cultural framework.

Raymond Williams has argued that the notion of hegemony allows us to go beyond the notion of 'culture', "in its insistence on relating the 'whole social process' to specific distributions of power and influence". Its forms of control are not only those usually seen as 'manipulation' or 'control', but are played out in "a lived system of meanings and values – constitutive and constituting – which as they are experienced as practices appear as reciprocally confirming" (1977: 110). The dominant culture "at once produces and limits its own forms of counter-culture"(114).

The tendency to valorise the 'indigenous' has only led to a refusal to understand culture in terms of its silences and distortions. A less romanticised notion of tradition and culture, which aims to interrogate their complicity with structures of power and domination, forms the basis of a number of critical historical studies in the Subaltern volumes.[10]

With the infusion of poststructuralist insights into some of these studies, culture is no longer regarded as a coherent and immutable system of signs and meanings. Rather, it is conceived of as an arena of struggle and change, where change itself is understood as a form of 'discursive displacement'. Gayatri Spivak (1987) has referred to critical reading as a way of understanding and promoting change, as 'an active transaction between past and future'. Struggle here is viewed primarily as a contestation over meanings. In Bhabha's contention, culture as a system of difference, and as a symbol-forming activity, is nothing other than 'a process of translations'.

This means that cultures are manifested in relation to the "otherness internal to their own symbol-forming activity"

making them "decentered structures" (1990c: 210-11). "Displacement" or "liminality", he argues, "opens up the possibility of articulating different, even incommensurable cultural
practices and priorities". Culture as a form of 'hybridity', in
other words, is a 'third space' that enables other discursive positions to emerge.

But as the notion of hegemony would suggest, it is a space
delimited or circumscribed by power. The conception of a third
space implies an already existing first and second space and of
boundaries, however nebulous, separating them. How are
these boundaries demarcated?

The distinctiveness of cultures and nations in various accounts, which depend upon a simple division of space, was referred to in the introduction to the book. Gellner, for instance,
defines nationalism as a

theory of political legitimacy which requires that ethnic boundaries
should not cut across political ones, and in particular, that ethnic boundaries within a given state ... should not separate the power holders from
the rest ... and therefore *state and culture* must now be linked. (1983:
1, 36; emphasis added)

Despite the virtual absence of such an ideal anywhere in the
world, the assumption continues concerning the co-incidence
of cultural boundaries of the 'nation' with the political boundaries of the state. This is indicative of the 'naturalising' effect
of the nationalist hegemony and its influence on ideological
apparatuses both in the realm of state and civil society. Absence of access to resources and exclusionary procedures can
thus enable the construction of minorities as deviants.[11]

Another problem is the premise that all members of a particular cultural collectivity are equally committed to that
culture. This leads to the construction of minority groups as
essentially homogeneous and monologic in their cultural
expressions, thus disallowing the possibility of internal dis-
agreements. In this sense, the idea of secularism (or cultural

diversity) posits an ahistorical, essentialist, fossilised unit of 'culture' with static boundaries. This underprivileges the shifting and fluid nature of cultural/national boundaries together with the narratives of collective cultural expressions. These narratives, Bhabha argues, co-exist with counter-narratives issuing from the community's margins voiced by cultural hybrids that live at the crossroads of more than a single culture. Such a hybridity summons up and at the same time blots out the totalizing boundaries of the community/nation.

The homogenising of the other and its cultural practices in colonial discourse finds continuity in the post-independent official discourse on culture. There seems to be an unquestioned assumption that all peoples spread over different parts of India, though culturally diverse at one level, ultimately belong to the same cultural universe and are therefore not very different from one another (cf. the Department of Culture's *Annual Report* 1985-86; 1990-91; 1991-92; 1992-93; 1993-94). Bhabha (1990a) has theorised a significant distinction between 'diversity' and 'difference', rejecting what might be called a version of multicultural liberalism where race, class and gender identities are based on a seemingly "transparent norm" or consensus imposed by the dominant group. In other words, the normative matrix that supports cultural diversity simultaneously orders and controls cultural difference: the "universalism that paradoxically permits diversity masks ethnocentric norms" (1990c: 208; see also Goldberg 1993). If in western multicultural societies this manifests itself as racism, then one could say that in the postcolonial context of India it appears as ethnic, religious, or regional discrimination.

THE HCR: EPISTEMIC CONTINUITIES

The text of the *Haksar Commission Report* (1990) can be seen as an attempt to establish leadership in the field of state-patronised culture (and, more tangentially, cultural practices beyond the jurisdiction or control of the state) through the reform of government policy towards cultural institutions (2-4). In critiquing the functioning of some of these institutions, it reproduces established norms rather than providing an alternative set of assumptions for a more broad-based and inclusive idea of 'Indian' culture. The central tactic of the document is to envision (and thus help materialise) a united pluralistic India, and then extrapolate from this harmonious polity a suitably unproblematic understanding of culture. In the utopian Indian society constructed in the text, tolerance and social harmony figure prominently vis-à-vis the manner in which differing cultural and ethnic groups are co-opted. The strains and tensions inherent in such cultural diversity are recontextualized in a mythical process of 'social change' that elides fragmentation and social conflict and, presumably, the operations of power.

The report lazily presupposes that it is not worth its while to question the dominant perception in the country of certain regions as being beyond the pale of official national culture. In this, it replicates age-old 'prejudices' which have guided Indian nationalist imagination in relation to 'peripheral' territories and cultures. Here is – to cite one example – Union Home Minister Sardar Patel writing to Nehru in 1950:

Our northern or north-western approaches consist of Nepal, Bhutan, Sikkim Darjeeling and the tribal areas of Assam. From the point of view of communication they are weak spots … . The contact of these areas with us, is by no means, close and intimate. The people inhabiting the portions have no established loyalty or devotion to India. Even Darjeeeling and Kalimpong areas are not free from *pro-Mongoloid* prejudices. (Quoted in *Himalayan Observer* 16(23), 1982; emphasis mine)

The 'us' above is unabashedly reproduced in the report when, while claiming a comprehensive, representative and cross-sectional view of the 'state of culture' in the country, it omits the entire region (cf. earlier discussion of Eliot's 'partial' or 'regional' cultures) from its project and thinks it fit to dismiss it with an apology:

We must express our deepest regret for not being able to visit the States of Arunachal Pradesh, Goa, Meghalaya, Mizoram, Nagaland, Sikkim and Tripura, and the Union Territories of Andaman and Nicobar Islands, Dadra and Nagar Haveli, Daman and Diu, Lakshadweep and Pondicherry. (Report 1990: 4)

Any delineation of culture(s) in these regions would of course import contradictions in the insular discourse of the document. In refusing to break away from the legacy of colonial anthropology, perceptions of peripheral regions have been allowed to ossify to an extent where, for example, a University Grants Commission team visiting the Centre For Himalayan Studies in North Bengal can unselfconsciously legitimise the Centre's sphere of activities on the following ('pro-Aryan') terms:

Although the basic objective of the Area Studies Centres is to study areas or regions other than India, the justification for the inclusion of the Indian territories that fall within the Himalayan range is that the people living there have very long and strong social and cultural affinities with those across the border (trans-Himalayan tribes) and a multidisciplinary study of the Himalayan states and peoples from India's point of view would require careful study of the ways and manners in which they influence people on the Indian side of the mountain and have been influenced by it. (Centre for Himalayan Studies 1986: 2-3)

This resonates with the observations contained in colonial reports about the cultural compatibility of the Himalayan peoples with those who live across the Indian borders rather than those found within the political and administrative boundaries of the country (India Office Records Eur D. 998/20). Before awareness about the cultural and economic intrusions of the plainsmen into the Himalayas grew, British interests largely viewed these regions (and, by extension, the 'peoples' and 'tribes' who resided there) either as a passage or obstruction to the smooth conduct of their trade activities across the mountain ranges[12] (India Office Records L/PS/20/D8).

The post-colonial Indian state, now armed with more sophisticated technologies of surveillance, polices ever more ag-
gressively the distinct cultural practices and boundaries of
these peripheral regions. Thus is born the idea of what one
writer calls, without irony, 'border management'. "For effective border management it is essential that the people staying
in border areas be firmly integrated with the rest of their
countrymen and function as the eyes and ears of the paramil-
itary forces/army entrusted with guarding the frontiers. Only
then will it be possible to effectively monitor our borders
without incurring infrastructural expenditure, which only di-
verts the precious resources of the country" (Liddle 1990:
204). Here we have a literal metonymic transference from the
body to the body politic.

While differences in history, language, location, etc., are admitted, and often celebrated, when it comes to abstract inter-
pretations of 'Indian Culture', this is achieved by eliding the
underlying contradictions, contrarieties and confusions. Official cultural discourse acknowledges such differences only to
reassert a unitary view that integrates all incompatibilities
within preconceived ideas about the cultural core. Predictably,
universal humanist platitudes are invoked to lend the appearance of veracity to this basic core and provide occasion for self-
congratulation:

We believe that as a result of this survey we have been able to secure an
integral view of the cultural scene in our country and a reliable insight
into the nature of the issues arising in the course of our review. (1990:
4; emphasis added)

In implying the existence (or building) of a common culture[13]
the report exercises the power to impose meaning; reinforcing
the grid through which otherness is defined.

Established as part of the 'national life' with the 'birth of
the nation', the Sangeet Natak Akademi, the Sahitya Akademi, the Lalit Kala Akademi, the National School of Drama and

other provincial and central bodies are considered to be the most prominent repositories of 'Indian culture'. The contributions of figures like Nehru, Radhakrishnan and Maulana Azad in the conceptualisation of Indian culture is noted, and the necessity of state intervention in the arts is argued for in conditions which have seen the disappearance of earlier modes of patronage through "durbars, courts, and religious bodies", keeping in mind the "limits and dangers of the market in regard to cultural creativity" (18). Linked to the political project of 'nation-building' – which is, in a large measure, a euphemism for the processes of homogenisation – the Akademis are expected to promote the moulding of a 'sensibility' which would "guide and reflect India's entry into modernity". Instead of questioning the apparent equation of modernity with nation-building, the report merely goes on to quote Nehru's speech at the inauguration of the National Arts Treasures Fund in 1955, in which he desired "every child of India" to "assimilate, even in a small measure, the genius of India, which adapted to modern conditions, should make the country grow" (19).

Together with the "growth" of the nation, the Akademis are linked to the larger context of a "revival" of culture. The report quotes Maulana Azad to the effect that "there has been a renaissance in India since the middle of the nineteenth century" but modifies the statement by explaining that the renaissance was "due to the release of new forces in society and owed little to the state". It then goes on to add the caveat that this autonomy is precisely the reason why the process of cultural revival "was not as extensive or deep as it would have been if it had received the necessary state support" (19). Despite the admission of a renaissance without state intervention, the report assumes that the state ("the organised manifestation of the people's will") alone can sustain the arts.

In making a case for state intervention in the field of the arts the report has to, of necessity, underplay if not overlook the production of art that survived and resisted colonial rule through various traditions of dissent. Although the upsurge of 'modernity' in the literary sphere is acknowledged, the same is done by reducing it to the efforts of a single pioneering figure (Tagore), implicitly negating the contribution of a large number of other writers. Similarly, the intervention of Indian cinema, for instance, and its mediations with industrial capital and the market, is completely ignored. The claim is made that modernity could not have come about without the direct intervention of the state or, more specifically, the Nehruvian administration.

At the same time, the institutional autonomy advocated by the government is reaffirmed in the rhetoric of the report: "We want to declare unmistakably that we are for less state control of art. We want art programmes to be administered by artists and not bureaucrats" (41). Official cultural discourse ever since independence is rife with statements about the necessity of art being kept outside the bounds of immediate state direction. In keeping with this tradition, the report cites S. Radhakrishnan as he spoke during the inauguration of the Sahitya Akademi:

You remember the remark once made by Napoleon: 'I hear there are no poets in France today. What is the minister of Interior doing about it?' The minister of the Interior can subsidise versifiers but he cannot create poets. Poets cannot be made to order. If we are to have creative literature in our country and not a managed literature, it is essential that the Akademi should remain completely autonomous. I am glad to know that Maulana Saheb who just gave it the first push, recognises that it will not be right for the government to interfere in the activities and the administration of the Akademi ... . (8)

Although no ministry of culture has been yet established, as yet some members of the intelligentsia feared, there is a department of culture that presides over the functioning of the Akademis. Thus, there is an exercise of political control, even as the absence of a ministry underscores the government's ostensible lack of responsibility for the arts.

This has led to a situation where there can be state interference even when there is little state support. Ironically, the report obliquely acknowledges this when it points to the contribution of the market: It "was the role of the market rather than the patronage of the state which set the pace for cultural endeavour after 1947" (21).

The report does not even begin to deal with the nature of the *relationship* between state and culture. An important omission, this lends to the text a degree of dubious coherence. Yet, owing to the ambitious nature of its aims, it ends up invoking a wide gamut of definitions in relation to 'culture' that, by its own admission, cannot be divorced from the state.

Culture is, the report reassures us, "what distinguishes human beings from other creatures in the process of natural selection" (7). The authority of an ancient Sanskrit source is invoked to assert that "without any sensitiveness to 'Sahitya', 'Sangeet', and 'Kala'", we would be "mere animals, even if they do not possess horns and tails". The repertoire of a cultured person would include 'traditional' qualities like *vidya, tapa, dana, gnyana, sheela, guna, dharma*. Occasionally, the word 'culture' is used interchangeably with *sanskriti* – although scholars are yet to confront the exact nature of the relationship – an identification that is being dangerously mobilised by fundamentalist forces in recent times. The problem of translation between the indigenous and western idioms is not one that admits of an easy solution and is one reason why any official discourse on cultural issues is often found wanting.

The report singularly fails to problematise the various usages of the terms to which it alludes. It makes, for instance, no attempt, while quoting him, to place in perspective the liberal view of culture that Nehru represented:

Does culture mean some inner growth in the man? Of course, it must. Does it mean the way he behaves to others? Certainly it must. Does it mean the capacity to understand the other person? I suppose so. It means all that. A person who cannot understand another's viewpoint is

to that extent limited in mind and culture ... the cultured mind should
have its doors and windows open. (9)

By excluding any historical context, meditations on culture can
only lead to vague generalities. Thus, the report tells us that
"diverse cultural activities" and "forms of artistic self-expres-
sion" (which is what 'culture' means in its "most comprehensive sense") generate "reflective poise" and "spiritual energy"
so essential "to the maturing of the good society" (6). What its
vision of "the good society" is, is never indicated. Generalities,
of course, have to be employed at times; but the ahistorical
generalities that the report employs occlude the workings of
power and impose a violent unity on manifest difference.

The question of whether the nation should be a culture-
oriented state or a state-oriented culture is a significant one
(Nandy 1988). The primacy accorded in India to the state in
this equation since colonial times is probably what generates
some of the problems encountered in the report. Because, as
Sudipto Kaviraj emphasises, "All societies have 'structures'
and states have to obey their logic, and adapt to its compul-
sions" (1991: 73). What the nature of these structures might
be can only be highly contentious; one could arguably speak
of a class structure, the caste structure, or structures in terms
of different communities.

Given the impossibility of a normative definition of
'nation', the attractiveness of Benedict Anderson's notion of
nation as an "imagined community" (1983) becomes apparent. The task facing the critic in examining any official discourse on national culture is to explain the process of how a
particular dominant imagination comes into being at the ex-
pense of others. One way of doing this is to look at the 'performative' everyday imaginings of the nation which take place
not from the centre but from the outside, the fissiparous margins. If 'nation' involves the division between 'us' and 'them',
and if it is imbricated in differential identity formation (as in
outside/inside), then it is not so difficult to understand the

imaginary power of hierarchizing the good 'mainstream' citizen over the not so good marginal one. It is worth pursuing the aspect which engages with what Bhabha calls "the complex strategies of cultural signification and discursive address that function in the name of 'the people' or 'the nation' and make them the subjects and objects of a range of social and literary narratives" (Bhabha 1990b: 292). That, I believe, could serve as an important element in the formulation of a critical historical and cultural studies programme.

My discussion of the *Haksar Commission Report* in particular demonstrates how its evasions, silences and generalities operate to install a notion of 'the people' and 'the nation' guaranteed by a 'neutral', and thus incontestible, objectivity.

A Digression on the Discourse of Development

It is beyond the scope of the present work to scrutinise the historical constitution of development, the process whereby the assemblage of conditions and conducts in the 'Third World' became defined as a problem "by making statements about it, authorising views of it, describing it, by teaching it, settling it, ruling over it" (Said 1979: 3).[14] Like the official discourse on culture, the developmental discourse is circumscribed in a way where only certain statements concerning capital, resources, technology and their interrelationship are allowed: "Once established and institutionalised, this set of statements determined from the outset what could be said, thought, imagined: they defined the space of development. Industrialisation, 'Green Revolution', family planning, macroeconomic policy, all refer to the same space, all repeat the same basic set of statements" (Escobar 1987: 15-16). Paraphrasing Foucault, this simply confirms the fact that the enunciative multiplicity of statements around a field only serves to define their regularity.

This discursive formation and its relationship with the non-discursive (or "the field of visibilities": socio-economic forces, political activities, institutions and so on) is such that development knowledge sustains the apparatus of development in a changing world by posing new problems. The apparatus or technology of development, in turn, goes on to translate in its practices the assignment thought out by knowledge in historicist terms. What is more, the field of visibilities provides fresh grounds from which new concepts can arise.[15] As Escobar argues,

[i]n the early post-war period, the "teeming" masses of the Third World attained a new visibility. Out of that new visibility, certain theoretical corpora (in economics, demography, science, agriculture, health and so on) conquered new realms of knowledge, new fields of statements. This field entered to enunciate problems and solutions in terms of "progress", the potentiality of science and technology, the preservation of freedom, the welfare of all humankind; in short, using a series of symbols that appealed to society, justice, rationality. (17-18)

It is instructive, too, to look at the implications that the knowledge-power continuum has in the process of dissemination. To quote Escobar again, development must be seen as

a pure function of power of an immense productivity: it circumscribes notions in certain ways, it effects socio-economic distributions, it produces orderings, sets of priorities (e.g., industrialisation and growth, etc.); and it does so by acting primarily on given sectors (agriculture, economics, population, etc.), fragmenting and recomposing them, creating and manipulating visibilities ("small farmers", "illiterate", "urban marginals", "informal sector", etc.), appealing to imperfections and insufficiencies (lack of capital, or of the right values, or of democratic institutions), actualising existing world forces (e.g., the market economy), and so forth. "Development" characterises the economy of power of the Third World, a situation in which they are, *themselves, the bearers and points of application of power.* (21; emphasis added)

One of the fundamental assumptions of development is the largely unquestioned trust in the force of modernisation to destroy old beliefs and archaic relations. The essential elements that go into the formulation of development theory are capital formation (which included factors like resources, technology, population, economic policies, trade, industrialisation, etc.), institutions (like national planning bodies), and cultural grounds such as education. The systematisations of the relations among these elements go on to constitute development discourse. These relations dictate the conditions that allow the emergence of certain concepts and objects.[16] This process, in turn, leads to the formulation of a policy.

Notes

1 An eminent Indian anthropologist has pointed out how much of "social science literature in India shares the assumption of the modern nation state" and vice versa (Das 1994: 138).

2 De Certeau in his *The Practice of Everyday Life* theorises the difference between 'place' and 'space' (1984: 29-42). Place, in simple terms, is the terrain where power is managed within its own boundaries. There is here a strong sense of possession and policing of power. Space, however, is the transgressive creation of the powerless whereby deviance and subversion can take place within the demarcated place managed by the powerful.

3 The political salience of such inquiries has not always been the same during different historical periods, whether in Britain or in India. As fact-finding and policy forming bodies, investigative committees begin to serve the function of institutionalising new state apparatuses in the first half of the nineteenth century. Not surprisingly, the changing nature of civil society in India has had certain effects. Commissions set up during colonial times had an aura of authority and power which commissions after independence have partially lost owing to the expansion of the public domain. In contradistinc-

tion to Europe where capitalism emerged in institutions within civil society, there was, in India, no developed civil society and the initiatives for capitalism's emergence were left to the state. (see Kaviraj 1991: 89; Freitag 1989).

4   In the second chapter I pointed out the hegemonic status of James Mill's *History of India*; as a text it shaped a whole body of opinion which imagined and ruled India (Inden 1990). Javed Majeed, in contrast, in a recent study argues that it was not really a hegemonic text. The liberal imperialism of Mill and the *History* was "first and foremost an attack on the ruling ideology [i.e.conservativatism] of the time" (1992: 195).

5   If one were to depend on a notion of 'the truth' or an unmediated access to 'reality', then the reality, as opposed to the ideology (where every one is free to do his/her own thing and choose amongst a plethora of lifestyles), of liberal societies would be more akin to this: "When one actually surveys the liberal reality, what one sees is more and more sameness – of tastes, of cliched perceptions of the world, of the glum ennui with which one reconciles oneself to the monolithic routines of our world. Needless to say, it is all too common for rhetoric of individuality to obscure a reality of dreary conformism. Such is liberalism, with its shopping mall culture – where one has hundreds of shops to choose from, all of which sell the same junk" (Beiner 1992: 23).

6   The word 'postcolonial' provokes a problem about historical periodization. It raises the question of how one negotiates spatio-temporal, psychic and phenomenological boundaries in a neo-imperial overdetermined formation. If it is to be productive, the post- is a way of conceiving the articulation of differences of identity, institutional position, geopolitical location, socio-economic determinants. For the postcolonial discourse theorist Bhabha, the notion of the post- is not the celebration of heterogeneity or bricolage but a certain kind of ex-centricity and expansion of instances of difference. The articulation of these instances of difference, which is not continually trying to achieve the state of totality, is suggested in *Nation and Narration* as a way of being able to "add to" without having to necessarily "add up".

7 Partha Chatterjee's seminal work (1986) on the discourse of third world nationalism has helped us understand that Indian nationalism, like other third world nationalisms, ails from sharing the same basic 'thematic' that underlies colonialist thought. Consequently, a radical critique of the latter is not available within a nationalist framework.

8 Nandy's claim here becomes a bit untenable. *If* it is continuous inflow and outflow which characterises India, then what of this idea of "determination"? Surely it does not apply.

9 This distinction between the state and civil society of course presupposes certain 'western-style' individualism. See, for instance, Hegel's criticism of Plato in *The Philosophy of Right* where he suggests that the latter's functionalism (incorporating slaves) does not sit well with the 'modern celebration of individualism'. See Taylor's *Hegel and Modern Society* (1979).

10 'Tradition', of course, is an embattled icon: "It is invented by a society's cultural vanguard in the course of a struggle. It marks off territories/identities of a named people as for example Indians. In that sense it is a loaded signifier drawing energy from an imaginary resource (the ideal tradition), but always remaining by virtue of its strongly ideological import an ambivalent, often culpable, sign in need of constant historical interpretation so that we know which way it is pointing" (Kapur 1988: 2). Thus for the Utilitarians, Indian tradition was the embodiment of evil, while for the Indologist (and the right wing political parties in India) it was the distilled essence of humanity.

11 The formal policy of secularism in India raises the theoretical problem concerning the 'legitimacy' of cultural differences. Which cultures, or strands of cultures, can be included in the secularist vision? Women's rights in Islam are taken care of by allowing a personal law (Hasan 1988). But the boundaries between private and public are socially determined and there is no easy way of guaranteeing them.

12 Sketching this history would take me off on a tangent, but for my purposes let me just cite S.K. Chaube who has summarised the felt need to 'Indianize' the Himalayas culturally as part of the nation-

building process: "Independent India has been confronted with a much more serious task than ordinary considerations of power politics or ideological cleavage postulate. That task flows from the broader problems of nation-building which India shares with her Himalayan neighbours" (1985: 2).

13 The invocation of a 'common culture', suggested, among others, by Gilroy (1987), obfuscates the ruptures and exclusions within it. In the British context, even the socialist appropriation of these concepts has reinforced the ideology of 'Englishness' which is racist, sexist, and culturally partisan. Paul Gilroy has taken even figures like Raymond Williams, Eric Hobsbawm, and E.P. Thompson to task for partaking in the naturalisation of racist modes of thinking. Theirs is a notion of patriotism dependent on 'one nation', which was particularly in evidence during and after the Malvinas war. Gilroy argues: "the suggestion that no one lives outside the national community is only plausible if the issue of racism is excluded. What is being described by these writers is a national community, not imagined in the way that Benedict Anderson has suggested, but actual. The construction of that community is overlooked. It is accepted a priori as the structure around which the struggle to gain hegemony must take place" (1987: 54).

14 To conflate the term 'discourse' in the two different senses in which it has been used, first, by Foucault who locates it within the institutional matrices of the modern episteme, and second, by Said who has a looser notion of it, is to disallow rigour. Aijaz Ahmad (1992) has argued that Said's use of the term 'discourse' to describe Orientalism is not historicized enough and has a broad sweep which includes within it representations of the East as they appear in Attic theatre or in times before the moment of colonialism. But it does not take away from my argument, even when I draw from Said, as I firmly stress the need to historicize and attempt to do so. Thus, early Orientalism, as has been forcefully suggested by Bhabha among others, is the dark side of European Enlightenment, when ideas of modernity and citizenship were being forged.

15 The discursive formation of development largely has an internal dynamics of its own. But does this discourse have autonomy of its

own? Foucault says that it necessarily does not: "If ... archaology ... refuses to see in discourse the surface of the symbolic projection of events or processes that are situated elsewhere, it is not in order to rediscover a casual sequence that might be described point by point, and which would make it possible to relate a discovery and an event or a concept and a social structure. But on the other hand if it suspends such a causal analysis, if it wishes to avoid the necessary connection through the speaking subject, it is not in order to guarantee the sovereign, sole independence of discourse; it is in order to discover the domain of existence and functioning of discursive practice. In other words, the archaeological description of discourses is deployed in the dimension of a general history; it seeks to discover that whole domain of institutions, economic processes, and social relations on which a discursive formation can be articulated; it tries to show how the autonomy of discourse and its specificity nevertheless do not give it the status of pure ideality and total historical independence; what it wishes to uncover is the particular in which history can give place to definite types of discourse, which have their own type of historicity, and which are related to a whole set of various historicities" (*Archaology* 1972: 164-65)

16 By the objects of development I mean population growth, poverty, agricultural practices thought to be primitive, lack of technology, cultural values, certain ethnic characteristics, etc. All of these were present before 1945 but not with such consistency and unity.

CHAPTER FOUR

'The Mirror is Empty'
Postcolonial English studies

In an interesting rumination on the discourse of a lecture, the French writer, intellectual and teacher Roland Barthes lays out the "gloomy" option that a lecturer has between the dominant habit of "conscientious functionary" and the mode of the "free artist". The second choice provides the space for the teacher to "get round" the anticipated official discourse; the price one pays, says Barthes, is to take in the reflected image of the "liberal" and "imperfect orator". The consolation, if any, is that at least one receives a reverberating image. The story most often is that "*the mirror is empty*" (Barthes 1977: 191-92; emphases mine). This, as the many who go to teach 'English' in the Indian classroom may recognise immediately, is the daily fate specifically of their profession: "the Other is always there *puncturing* his [the teacher's] discourse", for although silent, "the student audience ... *has an air* of not speaking – and thus, from the bosom of its flatness, speaks in you so much the louder" (195; emphasis in original). Overwhelmed with the day-to-day tasks of teaching, a large section of the English literature teaching community in India have become desensitized to this resounding 'silence', even when their tasks may include infusing poetic enthusiasm about daffodils when no student is likely to ever know what kind of flowers they are. But short of leaving their jobs "*en masse*" (Loomba 1989: 33) or calling for the abolition of English departments (Ngugi

1972), what options are there for teachers of English literature in a largely non-English speaking country like India?[1]

A sense of crisis about English studies in India is growing, reflected in the emerging debates within the discipline. This has led to a series of articles by those engaged in teaching and research in the subject.[2] These articles are the direct outcome of papers presented in two seminars held in India in 1988 and 1990. The first was held at the English Department, Miranda House, University of Delhi, and the second, 'Perspectives on the Teaching of English Literature in India', was jointly organised by the Centre for Linguistics and English, Jawaharlal Nehru University and the British Council Division, New Delhi. Another volume collects essays by crisis-aware academics under the title *The Lie of the Land* (1992). While these endeavours are striving to set the agenda for a reformed discipline at the university level, they constitute only the beginning for thinking about the problematic nature, scope and usefulness or otherwise of English studies in the country.[3]

My project also marks the first step in bringing together gleanings of diverse discourses that have 'created' the subject. I will draw from the efforts of these pioneering essays in the course of this chapter, but rather than pointing out the inadequacies or problems that I see in them,[4] my objective is to reinforce and to supplement the issues raised. From my perspective, the 'crisis' is in some ways akin to the one delineated in William Cain's *Crisis in Criticism* (1984). But the terrain in my case is a postcolonial space, and the problems of the profession, as of living, are of a distinct kind.

In the sections that follow I begin with the issue of the English language in the postcolonial moment; the debates revolving around language often touch upon those echoed in English literature. I then give a brief sketch about the sense of 'crisis' that is perceived in departments of English, both in the metropolis and in India. Next, I juxtapose that with the prevalent attitudes in these Indian departments in the following section. In keeping with the delineation of official discourse on education and culture that preceded this chapter, I then consider official reports that directly deal with the theme of teaching English. My final section is an implicit reading of *A Passage to India* through the eyes of critics who tend to either put forward an anti-imperialist Forster or depoliticise the novel. The analysis is intended to serve as a case study of the map of reading implicit in the Indian curriculum of English. This also allows me to argue in the conclusion of the book that canonized English texts can still have a place in a wider critical historical and cultural studies agenda.

ENGLISH: 'RAISE THE LID OF ... DESIRE'

In response to a question implicitly suggesting her imbrication in elitist and Eurocentric French theory, which she uses for her critique of imperialism, Gayatri Spivak makes a perceptive distinction. She sets apart her turn toward the West as a reaction to the 'command' of colonial and neo-colonial history from the West's desire for the non-West. Even though an intellectual constantly questioning her own disciplinary production, she cannot free herself from this matrix of the West's desire precisely because of the shared history of such production. Her strategy is thus to "raise the lid of this desire" by declining to be co-ordinated as the "true native" or to allow positing a "pure East". Any project arguing for "indigenous theory" to the exclusion of everything western, would only end up negating history (1990: 8).

There is an embedded parallel here with regard to the presence of English, the English language in particular, in independent India. Not only does a substantial amount of India's intellectual production take place in the medium of English (however transformed or 'deviant' a variety of it) but the language is also mired, as I detailed in the second chapter, in colonial history.

The role of English in the Indian national movement, as indicated in the earlier sections of the book, was less unequi-

Postcolonial English studies

vocal than that, say, in apartheid South Africa.[5] At one extreme was a revivalist response which bemoaned the decline and fall of 'Aryanism',[6] as articulated, for instance, by Pratap Narayan Mishra in an essay written in Hindi: "... you have poured everything into the fire of cigar while reciting the twenty-six letter mantra [i.e., of the English alphabet]" (quoted in Kumar 1991: 61). The other extreme was held by 'mimic' men like the early Michael Madhusudan Dutt who aspired to write like Milton, although later in his life he gave up writing in English altogether.[7] I do not want to dismiss 'mimic' men summarily, as to write in English was also a triumph;[8] and in some cases, as Bhabha would argue, a subversive act. The point here is that responses varied widely, and consequently the usage of English in itself took on a divisive significance within the movement.

The language also created a channel for ideas which were appropriated and used in the nationalist movements. Ambedkar's project of ensuring equality for the untouchables arose from within the liberal framework which reached India by the medium of college curriculum (see Chandra 1992). This curriculum was, in large measure, liberal in spirit in the texts chosen for the teaching of philosophy, political economy and English language and literature.[9] English as a *vehicle* of liberal ideas from England, no doubt, fired the imagination of the nationalist elite.[10]

The ambiguities towards the language per se in the nationalist position lay in the homonymy between colonialist and nationalist discourses. While English helped bring independence, it also stayed on to inflect the whole notion of independence: hence the term 'postcolonial', instead of 'postindependent', to allude to post-1947 events, ideas, configurations. Furthermore, as discussed in the second chapter, the beginnings of cultural nationalism in the last decades of the nineteenth century led to the emergence of figures like Bankimchandra who, as Partha Chatterjee (1986: 54-81) shows, began to understand that the forging of a nationalist discourse would not be possible without negotiating with the Enlightenment's 'cunning of reason'.

Implicit in the usual banal explanations of the role of English as a link language in a multilingual nation-state or its status as a library language, is the inseparable issue of modernization in relation to Indian identity.[11] Marx and others have held that British rule in India was a liberal humanist extension and deployment of the Enlightenment into that undiscerning backwater (see Marx and Engels 1959). For Nehru, the critical modernist,[12] it was the archaic, feudal, reactionary face of England that ruled over India. Nehru's concern about the presentness of the past in India's drive towards modernity is an anguish that haunts him in his search for answers in *The Discovery of India*: "We in India do not have to go abroad in search of the past and the distant. We have them here in abundance. If we go to foreign countries it is in search of the present. That search is necessary, for isolation from it means backwardness and decay" (1974: 565). That search for the present to avert isolation lay partly in English as a 'window to the world'.

The problem gnawing at the move towards Indian modernity for Nehru is "due to ... [the] arrested growth and the prevention [i.e. during colonial rule] by British authority of normal adjustments taking place" (507). This perception of anti-modern features in British policy in India makes him postulate a split in England. "Which of [the] two Englands came to India? The England of Shakespeare and Milton, of noble speech and writing and brave deed, of political revolution and the struggle for freedom, of science and technical progress, or the England of the savage penal code and brutal behaviour, of entrenched feudalism and reaction?" (287). He hypothesizes an ambivalent Janus-faced co-existence in his answer: "The two Englands live side by side, influencing each other, and cannot be separated; nor could one of them come to India forgetting completely the other. Yet in every major action one plays the leading role, dominating the other, and it was inevitable that the wrong England should play that role in India and should come in contact with and encourage the wrong India in the process" (288). Nehru is attempting to articulate, to manipulate, in Bhabha's terms, the "space between enunciation and address", between the western sign and its colonial signification. In this space emerges "the map of misreading that embarrasses the righteousness of recordation and its certainty of good government" (1994: 945).[13]

In his vision of a good Indian government and his efforts to build a single unambiguous national face with "normal adjustments", Nehru (and all those he spoke and acted for) allows, as Probal Dasgupta has argued,

India's nineteenth century relationship with the English of the humanities, plus the ideology of spiritualist-idealist nationalism, [to give] … way to a materialistic and scientific reading of the modernity narrative. The technical rudder of planning passes into the hands of a utilitarian communicative medium, of an English which controls the academic and juridico-constitutional discourse that defines developmental goals as well as the strategic and administrative discourse that allocates and deploys the resources to meet these targets. (1993: 166)

While India's relationship with the English of the humanities is far from a non-contentious one, and in need of extended historical research, Dasgupta makes a useful point in understanding the largely unacknowledged state patronage of the language. Sudipto Kaviraj (1990) has also delineated the passage of this 'rudder of planning' into the discursive space defined by English. Kaviraj has argued that the appropriation of English for India's technocratic planning belied the role of Hindi in the mobilization of the masses during the struggle for freedom. The work of the Congress Party which was earlier carried out in Hindi and on a politics based on Hindi switched over in the 1940s. This is evidenced in the Congress Working Committee meetings set up to deal with planning and nation-building. Technocratic expertise in and through

English was requisitioned for building up a techno-bureau-
cratic regime which the party would oversee in the industrial-
ization of the nation.

Nehru's 'passive revolution' which relied on nation-building ideals such as democracy, socialism, secularism, econom-
ism, planning, etc., (see Parekh 1995) also implied the need for
the English language for the achievement of developmental
goals. With the establishment of the Nehruvian state, English
specifically became a "clinical instrument of what is presented
as a temporary operation – a special state-sponsored acceler-
ation of the development process" (Dasgupta 1993: 166). It
was 'instrumental' in that there was a total reliance on English-speaking experts from the areas of science, technology
and management. This elite necessarily distanced itself from
any public debate (which would involve the participation of a
population that speaks 'other' languages) so that the state
could move on unimpeded in its plans.[14] In the absence of any
move to establish a broader public arena where a modernity
with a different trajectory could be defined, this elite "is struc-
turally compelled to represent itself to itself as an elite whose
modernizing mission is some sort of legacy or patrimony
which is continuous with the imperial modernizing endeavour
of the British Raj in the time dimension and with the global
developmental project of the Americans in the space dimension" (Dasgupta 1993: 167).

An allied question that crops up in this context is the manifest attitude of the Indian state concerning English. English
was to be phased out, a promise laid out in the Constitution,
as an official language after fifteen years. Hindi was to displace
it at the centre and the regional languages in the states. The
keeping of English, as evidenced in the *Constituent Assembly
Debates*, was far from unanimous.[15] The Hindi adherents had
to put off their zealous aspirations in the face of what seemed
to be a reasonable compromise. This is reflected in the prefat-
ory remarks of Gopalswami Ayyengar's resolution:

We could not afford to give up the English language at once. We have to keep the English language going for a number of years until Hindi could establish for itself a place, not merely because it is an Indian language, but because as a language it would be an efficient instrument for all that we have to say and do in the future and until Hindi established itself in the position in which English stands today for Union purposes ... We consider it very fundamental that English shall continue to be used in the Supreme Court and the High Courts until Parliament after full consideration, after Hindi has developed to such an extent that it can be a suitable vehicle for law-making and law interpretation, comes to the conclusion that it can replace the English language. (Constituent Assembly Debates n.d.: 1318-1320)

The doubts and fears raised over the proposed successor to English – i.e. Hindi – grew as it gained state assistance to the extent that Nehru's government (and governments after him) assuaged regional sentiments by promising that the 'temporary use' of English would continue indefinitely. Articles 210, 345, 346, 347 of the Constitution contain policy statements on the use of regional languages in state legislatures and other domains. Article 347, for example, states that if the President "is satisfied that a substantial proportion of a state desires the use of any language spoken by them to be recognized by that state [he may] direct that such languages shall also be officially recognised throughout that state or any part thereof for such purpose as he may specify" (Basu 1950).

The official attitude so far as education was concerned, seemed to favour vernaculars: the *Report of the University Education Commission* (1949) recommended that Indian students learn a regional language, a general language (Hindi), and English. The *Commission for Secondary Education* in 1953 further broadened the space for vernacular education by recommending the teaching of five languages. And later the Council for Secondary Education (1956) came up with the infamous three-language formula. The silence in these documents about a national language has effectively meant the continuance of English as the dominant medium. The fact that access to English education is restricted only to a few, however, suggests an inherent anti-development movement that generates precisely within the ostensible project of national integration around development goals.

In this context it should be mentioned that in northern India, a revivalist politics in opposition to English has become organized especially under the rubric of parties like the Bharatiya Janata Party (which came to power in some of the states there) and allied groups like the Vishwa Hindu Parishad and Bajrang Dal. This is separate from the recent movements in the states of Bihar and Uttar Pradesh (the lead of the Chief Minister Mulayam Singh Yadav in this context is noteworthy) to replace English with Hindi. These movements speak for the interests of the rural regional elites against the power of the English educated urban class, which self-consciously thinks of itself as the 'Builders of Modern India' for whom English, as Sheth has argued, is instrumental "for promoting the noble causes of development and national integration": "[t]hose who fail to share this altruistic logic, in its view, a 'national perspective' are victims of such dreaded and atavastic ideologies as regionalism, traditionalism and obscurantism" (1995: 190).

A postcolonial perspective that can transcend the constitutive binaries of urban-rural, metropolitan-indigenous, would therefore recognise postcolonial India's hybridized space so as to evolve a national policy on English based on universal access.[16] And here, English does not necessarily refer to any standardised version from Britain or the U.S.A., but an 'Indian English' (Kachru 1989), a hybridized linguistic product, that would be in keeping with the earlier selective absorption of Sanskrit and Persian in Indian history.

As pointed out earlier, the ambivalence that characterizes the reception of English can be explained by the psychic response of the colonized to the colonizer's language, and it is not necessarily always debilitating. In contradistinction to

Said who argues in *Orientalism* that power and discourse is possessed entirely by the colonizer, Bhabha theorizes an ambivalence at the site of the text's reception by the colonized (see Parry 1987: 40). "It is always in relation to the place of the other", Bhabha shows, "that colonial desire is articulated" (1980: xv).[17]

SENSE OF A CRISIS

What is the relationship between the rise of literary and cultural theory in the United Kingdom and United States, the consequent sense of a crisis in institutions in these places, and the appearance of unease in some select departments of English in Indian universities? The answer can at best be speculative, but my discussions thus far have suggested a historical connection as well as one in terms of a global cultural economy. The crisis I am referring to stems from the questions of what the discipline of English literature is, and what it is expected to do. Thus, we have Svati Joshi, the editor of the volume *Rethinking English: Essays in Literature, Language, History*, speaking for academics involved in the teaching of English: "Our growing sense of dislocation within our discipline and an even greater sense of bedevilment at the contradictions and crises of the time we are living in have left us with many questions concerning our academic engagement and its relation to our historical situation as well as the nature of political and cultural processes on our contemporary society" (1991: 1). The assumption – based on cultural materialist arguments – is that literature cannot be seen to embody universal values; it has to be seen historically.[18]

The notion of crisis is not new to the discipline in the metropolis. One way of narrating the emergence of English as a discipline is to argue that it was cultural and socio-political crisis in mid-nineteenth century England that brought about the beginnings of English departments. The coming into visibility of a schooled proletariat in the course of the nineteenth cen-

tury, which coincided with the erosion of the moralizing vector of religion, provided the space for a liberal humanist (with
conservative inclinations) programme to find in English literature the common humane values thought necessary to ce-
ment the social formation together (Eagleton 1983).[19]

Paul Bové also draws upon this mode of political analysis in
his *Intellectuals in Power* (1986). His book is an institutional
history that stresses the importance of a radical rethinking of
the relations between literary studies and power relationships
in the wider realm. Other studies, like that of Gerald Graff's
"institutional history" (1987) of literary studies in American
universities, focus on conflicts that were marked by depart-
mental structures. The focus here, however, is on the expansion of literary education; Graff does not question the whole
enterprise.

Ideological critiques of literary study have importantly ex-
posed the relations between English studies and the capitalist
state but have remained moored in abstraction. As Paul Bové
remarks: "It [i.e. critique] operates at too high a level of gener-
ality to catch the specifics of particular material and discursive
situations" (1986: x). Ian Hunter also points out how critiques
neglect to investigate "the way in which different arrays of
human capacities and aptitudes are formed through historically specific cultural techniques and institutions" (1987: 299).

Another way of looking at the emergence of the discipline
is to locate oneself with Viswanathan (1989) who, as mentioned in the second chapter, points out that English literary
studies were launched in India before they appeared and became established in the British university curriculum. In the
interests of the empire, knowledge about the Orient travelled
to the West while English literary studies went to the colony
in the East. The functions that English studies came to serve
in England was, as expected, not the same as they did in India.
Brian Doyle's study shows that in England, "before 1880 most
teaching of languages and literature was either associated with
women, or allied to the utilitarian pursuit of functional liter-

acy, and therefore occupied a dramatically lower cultural status than the upper-class masculine studies of Classics and Mathematics" (1989: 2). English studies in the colonies served to stand for the aura and mystique of classical studies in Greek and Latin. This transference of low status symbolic material from the metropolis was presented as the high form of English culture which the colonized could and should strive for.

That there are various ways of mapping the emergence of English literature only serves to establish that there was a degree of ambivalence in its birth; and that the presence of a 'crisis' was never very far away. What concerns us, when we talk about its function, its contours, its canonized (albeit changing) identity, is its imperial connection; that it came into being in a certain socio-historical juncture; and that it attempted to define itself by universalization of the values it claimed to embody.

English Department: 'Calcutta Mill'

Two central questions that suggest themselves here are: (i) What is taught in English departments in the Indian universities and/or their affiliated/constituent colleges? and (ii) What are the objectives of literary studies? More specifically, the first question asks in what ways does the de-relativising, ruminative and deliberative discipline, with its defining site in the U.K. (and more recently, the U.S.A.), interact with the terrains and tempos of contemporary India? As the *Report of the Curriculum Development Centre in English* (1989) uncritically puts it, "In most universities, the basis for classification of papers/courses seems to be the following: (i) Genre (e.g., Marathwada, Jodhpur); (ii) Chronological/ periodwise (e.g., Bombay, South Gujarat). In several universities, some courses are based on themes or individual authors" (21). A look at syllabi and examination papers of universities in Calcutta, Bombay, Shillong, Rajarammohunpur, and others suggests that the reigning paradigm is comfortably drawn from Arnold, "the best that is known and thought in the world" (1965: 58) (high seriousness); Leavis (moral substance, concrete experience, formal coherence);[20] and the New Critics ("well-wrought urn", "verbal icons", which are complex, ironic, paradoxical, subtle, dehistoricised words on a page).

Recent moves in those universities which are more familiar with critical fashions to incorporate deconstruction as a reading strategy, have only resulted in extending the New Critical enterprise.[21] The 'useful' Derrida, wrenched out of all contexts, is the one who is reduced to being the author of 'there is nothing beyond the text'. To the extent that one can infer from articles published in Indian journals, we can say that there is no attempt to set up a relationship between text and context (the way that most western-based feminists and other cultural critics have done) to redefine the boundaries between academia and the outside world. I am not arguing for a direct connection between literature and socio-political conditions; I am suggesting that, while concerned with the theory/practice tension (i.e. in terms of aesthetic value/political ideology opposition), the mimetic significance of intervention, when the contextual slides into the textual, cannot be under-priviledged. Literature does not provide unmediated access to socio-political conditions. Languages and social practices, as Voloshinov (1986) echoing Saussure, has shown, mediate what we refer to as reality. The distinction between theory and practice – if thought of as being mutually exclusive – is false (Derrida 1986: 167-69). Gadamer makes much the same point when he stresses the moment of application, along with interpretation, as integral to understanding in hermeneutical experience (1982: 274-75).

Theory is, in fact, politically redefined by Derrida when he famously says that 'there is nothing beyond the text'. His sense of 'text' is an uncircumscribed one which, when misread, misses out the implications it has for theory and criticism. When charged with the questionable usability of his textual strategy, Derrida clarifies:

... text, as I use the word, is not the book. No more than writing or trace, it is not limited to the paper which you cover with your graphism ... for strategic reasons ... I found it necessary to recast the concept of text by generalising it almost without limit ... .That's why there is nothing 'beyond the text'. That's why South Africa and apartheid are, like you and me, part of this general text, which is not to say that it can be read the way one reads a book. That's why the text is a field of forces: heterogeneous, differential, open and so on. (167-68)

The recent appropriation of Derrida and some other literary theorists has served to privilege the primacy of the text understood in a narrow sense (see, for instance, Singh 1989; Jain 1989). In general, either there is an outright rejection of structuralism and poststructuralism (see Chapter One; also Narasimhaiah 1993: 19-22) or the deployments of contemporary literary theory, on the whole, are rare.[22]

The across-the-board assumption in all the narrowly textual modes of reading and critical practices that are prevalent in India is that English departments should only be involved with 'great literature', or more precisely the 'great tradition' of English literature beginning from around Chaucer and breaking off after the 1920s or 30s with T.S. Eliot (see *Report of the Curriculum Development Centre in English 1989*: 345-61).[23] "Liberal assumptions about English literature as 'universal' and 'normative', and orthodox critical methods that deny any possibility of connecting the English text with our material world", writes Svati Joshi, a teacher of English in a New Delhi college, "continue to inform much of our pedagogical activity" (1991: 1; see also Loomba 1989: 10-37).[24] Examination questions generally call upon examinees to elaborate upon a theme or comment on a character or ask for a formal analysis of a set poem, play, or novel. This emphasis on the text, pedagogically speaking, reifies the text's autonomy (see Hill and Parry 1994); that the 'truths' embodied in it must be relativized by contextualization becomes unnecessary and even undesirable.

The passivity that this canonical mode induces in the reader was recognized as early as the beginnings of the discipline by Walter Raleigh, the first really 'literary' Professor of English at Oxford. In his first post as Professor of English Literature at the Anglo-Oriental College in Aligarh, where his job was "implementing Macaulay's cultural crusade in India", he discovered that his task was the 'Calcutta Mill': simply "to cram a well worn subject into a given number of unfilled heads" (quoted in Baldick 1983: 76). Such a policy of 'saturation' is still advocated and practised in the classroom today, as Sunder Rajan reports in her article dated 1986.

British literature forms the "common core of the MA programme in all the universities: ranging from 3 out of 8 papers (e.g., Marathwada, Gujarat) to 7 out of 8 papers (e.g., Calcutta)" (*Report 1989*: 21). There are a few universities that have a less rigid syllabus. The consensus is broken here in that optional courses (or papers as they are more commonly referred to in India) in linguistics, Indo-Anglian, Commonwealth literature, and now even samplings of literary theory have been introduced.[25] But the spirit of 'accommodation' ensures that the core remains metropolitan in character. Mulk Raj Anand, Raja Rao, R.K. Narayan, Nissim Ezekiel, Keki N. Daruwalla, A.K. Ramanujan and some younger writers may increasingly appear in the courses, but they do so as Indian Others hitched to the canon-wagon of the European Subject. And this expansion comes mostly in the form of optional courses (as is evident in the way they are appended at the end of university syallabi) which often serve to appear to be proffering variety, while continuing with the live and firing canon. Indian writing must, more often than not, go begging, at the cost of wasting its potential power to challenge the whole issue of tradition and the question of its location in culture, and of culture in the social formation, which would then demand ideological analyses and historical understandings.

An instance of how this happens is the criticism of eminent academics like C. D. Narasimhaiah and Srinivasa Iyengar who represent the nationalist turn in English studies. A pioneering spokesman for the Indian writing in English, Narasimhaiah makes an impassioned plea in his celebrated *The Swan and the Eagle* (1966) for a level of writing (in English) that is at par with the finest produced in the metropolis. At the same time he denounces what he considers to be the "shameless jingoism" of those nationalists who (presumably like Ngugi Thiong'o) argue in favour of writing in the vernacular languages. Narasimhaiah's argument is simple: "He is a poor writer indeed who chooses to write with a view to serving any of these for, according to W.B. Yeats, a poet by serving his art with utter integrity serves the nation also" (1966: 7). His mode of argument for the support of Indian literature in English depends, not unlike the Chatterjeean thematic of nationalist thought, on the invocation of the English literary canon. Thus, as an exponent of R.K. Narayan, he says: "Narayan's sense of the comic is sustained not only by the Dickensian kind of exaggeration but rather, if a comparison has to be made to enlist understanding and evoke response, the irony of understatement practised by Jane Austen" (139). The question that immediately comes to mind is: whose 'understanding' needs to be enlisted? Who constitutes the readership of the work? Is he just trying to sell writers like Narayan abroad? Or are his addressees those 'shameless jingoists'? In which case, there is no need to sell anything.

The objectives of literary studies, and English literature in particular, is another area of contention which needs to be addressed. Dismissing the obviously English nationalistic claim that English literature should be taught because it is 'the best', H.G. Widdowson has put forward two possible reasons for teaching it: "[t]hese reasons relate to the two ways of interpreting the term 'English Literature'. One may interpret it as meaning the literature of England including (by courtesy) Ireland, Scotland and Wales and perhaps even the English-speaking countries of North America and the Antipodes. The reason for teaching English Literature in this sense would be essentially a cultural one: to acquaint students with ways of looking at the world which characterise the cultures of the English- speaking peoples ... ." He goes on to suggest the other way of interpreting the term is to gloss it as "'Literature written in the English language'. On this interpretation, the reason for teaching it would be to acquaint students with the manner in which literary works in English use the language to convey special meanings" (1975: 77-78). Widdowson ultimately rejects the teaching of it on a cultural basis, as that "might after all best be taught by using material other than literature" and he opts for English literature as "an inquiry into the way a language is used to express a reality other than that expressed by conventional means" (80).

The aim of literary studies as they are currently being taught in India is certainly not to inculcate in students an awareness of the divides and issues concerning high art and popular culture, European Subject and Indian Other, liberal individualism and materialist commonality, practice and theory. This is again clear from the questions asked in examinations (see, for instance, *English-T.Y.B.A Exam 1994*, University of Bombay; *English M.A. Exam (Part I & II)*, University of North Bengal).

An adequate engagement with the question of the objectives of teaching English literature would necessarily demand the expansion of English to include other Indian literatures. Since my project does not have that kind of reach, I will in passing make a few observations about the implication of Indian literature and language pedagogy in the same orientalist discourse that defines the study of English (a discourse which, as we spelt out in the second chapter, includes the liberal Anglicist project in its wider application). Orientalist perceptions of 'Indian literature' are not separate from the European understandings of what materials qualify for the status of literature and the devices and strategies developed to study it. A "foundational knowledge" about India is set in order through the grid of orientalism (Dharwadker 1993; Ludden 1993). Its

representational project comes to form an essentialist and tot-
alist discourse on literature which is seen as a manifestation of
the 'genius' of Indian society.

The broad concept of literature (in a manner close to the
conceptions of 'text' and 'discourse') that was used by Indologists like William Jones (1786), to refer to all the known and
existing texts in a particular language (mostly Sanskrit), was
not applied to other Indian languages.[26] "In fact", writes Dharwadker, 'they reserved the comprehensive definition of literature for very specific purposes: the ancient Hindu-Sanskrit
world, and the Sanskrit-Pali-Tibetan Buddhist world" (168).
This made possible the exclusion of large areas of texts in the
literatures of modern Indo-Aryan and Dravidian languages.[27]
With this went the deprivileging of existing vernacular traditions so that the need for the creation of a national literature
for India could become urgent.[28]

It has been established that although there was no dearth of
such a literature, Indologists ignored it (see Tharu and Lalitha
1991). Trevelyan, as indicated in the second chapter, had referred to "the almost total absence of a vernacular literature,
and the consequent impossibility of obtaining a tolerable education from that source only" (1838: 23). English thus was to
provide the necessary impetus for forging a national literature. The languages of India will be assimilated by the languages of Europe, just as:

[t]he vernacular dialects of India, will, by the same process, be united
amongst themselves. This diversity among languages is one of the
greatest existing obstacles to improvement in India. But when English
shall everywhere be established as the language of education, when the
vernacular literature shall everywhere be formed from materials drawn
from this source, and according to models furnished by this prototype,
a strong tendency to assimilation will be created. Both the matter and
the manner will be the same. Saturated from the same source, recast in
the same mould, with a common science, a common standard of taste, a
common nomenclature, the national languages as well as the national

character will be consolidated ... . We shall leave a united and enlightened nation where we found a people broken up into sections ... and depressed by literary systems, designed much more with a view to check the progress, than to promote the advance, of the human mind. (1838: 124-05)

Trevelyan's writing on the education of the Indian people finds an echo across a century in the presidential address of the nationalist professor Amarnath Jha when he argues for the development of an indigenous literature through immersion in and close study of English literature: "The correlation of Western and Hindu canons of criticisms is a task which can be performed only by the scholars of English working in the country" (1941: unpaginated).

In a British Council seminar organised in 1961 on the teaching of literature overseas, Macaulay's cultural crusade in India for forging a national culture is reiterated in the speech of the highly influential professor V.K. Gokak (1963). An ardent enthusiast of Indian literature, he sees literature as being "as much an expression of universal man, of 'eternal verities' as it is of the manifold stages in the life of a society or a nation". English literature has captured the grandeur of "the theatre set for the evolution of the individual, of humanity, through the ages". From this timeless perspective, the inseminative power of that literature enters into his own nationalist realm where it will invigorate and renew the Indian literary tradition. As a believer in the 'stages of growth' model normalized by development discourse, he goes on to remind students of English literature in developing countries that they should be conscious of the axiom that:

their study will be invaluable to them if they choose to become pioneers in a national culture. But there is also the likelihood that they may come under the spell of 'La belle Dame sans Merci' and be held in her thraldom forever ... . In that case they will be a lost generation, like the Indians in the fifties of the last century, who thought they lived in a desert, … remembered with avidity … every detail in the topography of *Thyrsis* and *The Scholar Gypsy*, but not the landscape pictured in *Kalidasa's Meghaduta* or the name of the sage who educated Rama and his brothers … . (unpaginated)

The transformation of the desert into a garden can come about, Gokak asserts, through an assiduous pursuit of English literature. The development of an indigenous literature and the making of a national culture is thus wholly dependent, according to Gokak, on the deployment of what is for him the transformative power of English literature.

Translations of 'suitable' works and writing of original literary works were encouraged and pursued as the proliferation of novels and translations during and after "the fifties of the last century" suggests.[29] These writings, at least according to one critic, are mostly the expressions of "minds saturated with English knowledge and tastes formed by the study of English masterpieces" (Mayhew 1926: 85). Thus, as Tharu points out, "[n]ovels and shorter fictional pieces apparently intended for women contrasted a bad woman, nearly always a Hindu, with a good woman who had either become a Christian or accepted Christianity's civilizing humanist essence" (1991: 168).[30]

Naipaul (1977), imagining India from what he considers to be the location of the modern 'outside' (as opposed to the traditional 'inside'), in a move reminiscent of orientalist perspectives, views current Indian literature (and by this he means literature written in English) as issuing from 'traditional' inspirations. Thus, novelists like R.K. Narayan, even though "one of the … best" (19) in Naipaul's argument, are incapable of handling the genre of the novel, simply because they are entrapped within the 'inside' of their traditions, and have no view from 'outside'.[31]

The distinction that Naipaul makes between the 'inside' and the 'outside' collapses in Spivak's reading of texts written in different locations (centre or periphery) and different times (colonial or post-colonial). Spivak, in her article 'The Burden

of English' (1993), examines the possibility of epistemic transformation through readings of English literary texts and
argues against linguistic nativism. By bringing together a
reading of Tagore's 'Didi' with Kipling's *Kim*, she argues that
the English teacher needs to unpack the artificial division
between English and vernacular literatures as they are fixed in
institutions. "It is particularly necessary today", she asserts,
"not to differentiate British and Indian literatures as 'central'
and 'marginal' in a benevolent spirit; that differentiation is a
mere legitimation by reversal of the colonial cliché whose real
displacement is seen in the turbulent mockery of migrant literature – Desani or Rushdie" (141-42).

Furthermore, through her twin readings of Binodini Dasi's
Amar Katha and Hanif Kureshi's *The Buddha of Suburbia*,
Spivak argues that we can construct an alternative literary
historiography (in the shift from coloniality to postcoloniality
to migrancy in the space of a century) if we "attended to the
fact that Binodini's imagined 'England' and the representation
of Karim's imagined 'India' are both 'created' under duress"
(1993: 149), without erasing the difference.

Official Reports: 'Field Coverage'

I now move on to consider the official position on the teaching of English in India. There have been a number of official
policy reports, including The Study of English in India by the
Ministry of Education, Government of India in 1967; and The
Report of the Study Group on Teaching of English produced
by the Ministry of Education and Youth Services, Government of India, New Delhi in 1971. These reports and their recommendations focus on the need for courses which will give
students a "thorough grounding both in language and literature", an "adequate command over the use of English and introduce them to a critical appreciation of English Literature"
(Report 1971: 30). They are mainly concerned about 'falling'
standards in English and present no notion about what 'crit-

ical appreciation' or 'English Literature' mean; nor do they express any doubt about the role of English in India.[32]

Keeping in mind the discussion on official discourse around English in colonial India in the second chapter, it is instructive to note the nature of the changes proposed in English courses in the 1989 *Report of the Curriculum Development Centre in English* brought out by the University Grants Commission, New Delhi. This report overtly links itself up with the *National Policy on Education: Programme of Action 1986* by quoting directly from it to indicate its own place in the wider national goal of keeping "pace with the fast-changing needs and demands of the society" (3). It goes on to cite *Challenge of Education: A Policy Perspective 1985* to endorse "a common core curriculum to strengthen *unity within diversity* and to facilitate mobility from one part of the country to another" (4; emphases added).

The report is in resonance with the *Kothari Commission Report 1964-66* and the *Haksar Commission Report 1991* (analysed in Chapter Three) in stressing the importance of making "education meaningful in the task of national development" (4). How does it strive to make "education more meaningful to the needs and aspirations of its beneficiaries as well as … socially relevant", with regard to English (4)?

At the post-graduate level, the Report has recommended a core of six papers comprising: English Literature from 1500 to the present day (four papers); Literary Criticism (one paper); and the Structure of Modern English (one paper). These are all to be compulsory papers so that a measure of uniformity across various MA English syllabi is provided in the country (33). Elective papers have been developed in the form of modules or groups. Depending on the annual system of teaching and examination and on whether a university has eight, nine or ten papers for study in the MA programme, a student can choose two, three or four papers (respectively) from an elective module (or group) of his (*sic*) choice. Each group has four to five papers listed under it. This has the effect of reducing the number of literature Core courses from eight to five to accommodate a 'structure of Modern English' course and specialisation courses – any two/three/four areas from the thirteen suggested. It is argued that several of these areas will prepare the ground for a change in the canon. The areas suggested are, for instance:

Group I: World Classics in Translation
            Apart from world classics, will include Vyasa and Valmiki in 'Epic', Buddhist *Jataka* tales, *Puranas*, *Katahsaritasagara*, *Panchatantra* and Tagore in 'Fiction', and Tamil *Sangam* poems, Iqbal, Tagore, Bharati and medieval *bhakti* poetry in 'Poetry'.
Group II: Modern European Literatures
            Includes literatures in French, Spanish, German, Italian, Greek, Yugoslav, Romanian, Polish, Czech and Hungarian.
Group V: Indian Literatures in English and English Translation
            Includes Bankim, Chandu Menon, Premchand, Tulsidas, *Sakuntala*, *Kadambari*, Surdas, Guru Nanak, and Indian Poetics (with Vedic philosophy and *Dhvanyaloka*).
Group IX: Special Studies
            Includes Women's Writing 1780-1980, Literature of Protest, literature of Utopia and Dystopia, and 'The Colonial Encounter'(39-42; 259-72).

Apart from this expansion of the canon, the real qualitative change proposed is the inclusion of Indian literatures in translation. The move is towards the addition of a comparative literature dimension. The changes in the prescribed texts are marked by the exclusion, for example, of Bunyan's *Pilgrim's Progress* (a text central in Alexander Duff's scheme of studies) and Bacon's *Essays*. Bacon's *Advancement of Learning* appears in its stead. In 'Literary Criticism', a considerable number of critics writing after Eliot have been included. Thus, for example, Eagleton's *Marxism and Literary Criticism* and Jameson's *Marxism and Form* have been included as 'recommended reading', even though they are not 'required reading' (Report 1989: 213). The shift in the function of literature here seems to be from Enlightenment to modernization. The shift towards a more flexible canon can be construed as intending to cater to what Colin MacCabe (1985) in his article, 'English literature in the global context', has called the "multicultural, multilectual present".

The thrust of my argument in this book is that the transformation of the existing canon through such curricular changes can, in a teaching-learning situation such as India's, achieve but little, especially because it operates within what might be called, following Graff, 'field-coverage'. Field coverage manifests itself through the option system that the Report valorizes and which is on the agenda in English departments as they open themselves more, especially to Indian literatures written in English. In his study *Professing Literature* (1987), Graff identifies field-coverage as a structural development that was instituted in the American system. This is a principle whereby the teaching of English is divided into fields, each taught independently by specialists, eliminating the conflict over first principles and the ideology of literature. Graff reveals that the field-coverage model came into existence in America in the late nineteenth century after the collapse of the College system and the fragmentation of the unified humanist ideology that had been propagated through an education based on the classics.

As a result of the critique of Eurocentric bias in the curricula and the question of the 'relevance' of English, field-coverage can, given the existing configurations in Indian departments of English, only get more established. Graff's description explains the usefulness of the model for English departments that were under threat of disintegration:

The field-coverage principle made the modern education machine fric-
tion-free, for by making individuals functionally independent in the
carrying out of their tasks it prevented conflicts from errupting which
would otherwise have to be confronted, debated, and worked through.
An invisible hand – fortified by the faith that humanism in the Mathew
Arnold sense pervaded all the branches of the departments and the
profession's activities – saw to it that the sum of the parts added up to a
coherent whole. (9)

The option system which the Report strongly recommends reproduces once again, in its emphasis on critical and reading
skills, the value in appreciating a selected number of texts
from an expanded, and to a certain degree 'Indianized', canon.
This can result not only in the neutralization of serious criticism but also in thwarting and co-opting the move, initiated at
the seminars mentioned at the beginning of the chapter, towards the 'radicalization' of discourse in English studies. My
own argument, of course, is to move beyond what they refer
to as 'radicalization', towards a more open discipline resem-
bling an historically critical cultural studies, the contours of
which I will suggest in the conclusion to my book.

FORSTER: 'FISSURES IN THE INDIAN SOIL'

The possibilities of enabling readings of canonized texts
through a comparative perspective was touched upon earlier
in the chapter. Here I will consider Forster's *A Passage to India*
from the standpoint of 'the place of the other'. I recall having
the choice, for my B.A. Honours examination in English literature, between answering either the question on *A Passage
to India* as 'essentially a novel dealing with the problem of
personal relationships' or to 'demonstrate the mystical dimension of the novel by commenting on the oum-boum of the
Marabar Caves'. While the questions betray certain institu-
tionalized modes of reading canonized texts and the privileging of ahistorical critical analyses over other methods, they

also raise further questions about the reception of Forster in India in the form of the text as embodying liberal ideals or his implicit critique of imperialism.

Recent accounts of the novel have seen it as "[a]nticipating Said's critique" and crediting Forster with "writing the ethnography of British colonialism in India" (Dirks 1992: 1-2). Jenny Sharpe, pitting the novel against the Mutiny of 1857, reads it "as a narrative that reveals the limits of an official discourse on native insurgency. It is a discourse that racializes colonial relations by implicating rebellion in the violence of rape" (1993: 221).

My contention is that these accounts are far too generous and that the novel can be examined as a subscriber to the liberal myth of imperialism, a way of seeing India which not only appropriates its nationalist movement but also neutralizes its alterity. Otherness is hollowed out so that an ideal that valorizes cross-cultural understanding among men may stand out.

By way of parenthesis, it should be reiterated here that the dominant explanatory paradigm of politics and history in modern India is to see colonialism and nationalism as antagonistic political ideas. The discourses of colonialism and nationalism, however, present in themselves a unity that historiography elides. The degree and significance of this unity has generated debate among scholars in Indian history and postcolonial literary theorists.[33] The critique is essentially to show that in the earlier dominant historiographies "issues are posed as India versus Britain" (Prakash 1990: 401). This bipolar division, Partha Chatterjee (1986) argues, serves to neutralize and negate the complicity between Indian nationalism and British imperialism. That is not to deny that nationalism challenged the imperialist notion of India, which saw Indians in terms of passivity, dependency, otherness. Nationalism, in its place brought with it the conception of India as active and sovereign; nevertheless it was mired in the intrinsic premises on which the negative ideas that buttressed imperialism were constructed. It bought into the same essentialist ideology that colonial knowledge used to objectify India. Bound up in modernity, it (like imperialism) valorized the ideals of reason, history, progress, as evidenced in the programmatic statements of the English curriculum. Imperialism's world-view which made East and West as distinct entities in terms of geography, culture, spirit, etc., corresponding and affirming post-Enlightenment taxonomy which had manufactured a transcendent knowing subject and a non-transcendent object of knowledge, was unwittingly harnessed by the nationalist project. "There is", argues Chatterjee, "consequently, an inherent contradictoriness in nationalist thinking, because it reasons within a framework of knowledge whose representational structure corresponds to the very structure of power nationalist thought seeks to repudiate" (1986: 38). India as an 'object' for the nationalists thus came into their vision as something to be mapped, to be elaborated. Indology which had been the preserve of the Europeans until then, now opened its discursive doors to the nationalists to allow them to produce their own programme of action, their own account of 'India'. Thus, in Chatterjee's reading, Nehru, at times, appropriated for his vision of an industrialized nation-state Gandhi's counter-modern, anti-progress views to win over the Indian people (see also Parekh 1995).

In the light of this historiographical digression, it is instructive to see how Forster's novel has been treated as a social and historical document for many years now. Indeed, it has often been taken as a barometer of the mood that defined Anglo-Indian relations in the early 1920s. His views of India have provided serious images and interpretation for Britain. Thus John Beer, writing in the foreword to G. K. Das's *E. M. Forster's India*, asserts that Forster's attitudes, found in his novel as well as his journalism on India, "helped to create the ground for the final cession of English power as it took place, by revealing to many politicians in England the shaky foundation on which that power had been built, and the need for a graceful retreat" (Das 1977: xiv).

Historians have also acclaimed Forster for his 'accurate' depiction of India. The kind of influence that he had on the British establishment in its view of India is enacted in the history of Indian nationalism, *India Today* (1942), authored by Duffet, Hicks, and Parkin. The authors cite Forster as evidence for their claim that "most British officials were unable to have any feelings of real friendship for their educated Indian associates" (1942: 71). Frances Singh and others have shown that Forster's novel is amenable to a historical appropriation for purposes of interpreting twentieth century Indian nationalism. In her study (1985) she draws parallels between the liberalism of Forster and the basic principles of Gandhian ideology, for example, by collating their political insights: "Forster and Gandhi ... both accept that chaos is constructive, that it will be the medium in which Indian independence will be born ..." (272).[34]

The tradition of seeing Forster as paralleling some of the anti-imperialist ideas then put forward by nationalist leaders puts him in contraposition to Kipling. Where Kipling disallowed the loosening of authorial monologic control over his narratives, Forster is lauded for his implicit dialogism by the critic Benita Parry: "Against the grain of a discourse where 'knowing' India was a way of ruling India, Forster's India is a geographical space abundantly occupied by histories and culture distinct from the Western narrative of the world and the meanings this endorses" (1985: 29). On the other hand, even while there is a reluctance to foreground the ambivalent borders of his anti-imperialism by critics even as sensitive as Parry, Forster's imbrication in the symbolic order of the political system he appears to impair is taken up for close scrutiny by some postcolonial critics.

Sara Suleri's essay, for example, is an insightful reinterpretation of *A Passage to India* which views Forster's text as "locating itself on the cusp between colonial and postcolonial narrative ... in its ability to demystify the mundanities attendant on colonial exchange" (1992: 144). Her earlier essay, 'The

Geography of *A Passage to India'*, describes the novel as one
of the first to introduce a narrative mode which superimposes
on the historic site of India a "vast introspective question
mark". In the production of this perfect modernist novel,
Forster has turned its subject (India) into an annex of the
"writing mind of the West" (1987: 169). Suleri displaces Kipling (regarded as the archetypal image-producer of India) with
Forster as the initiator of the colonialist cartography: "a text
like *Kim* in fact reinforces the reality of India by seeing it so
clearly as the other that the imperial west must know and
dominate. *A Passage to India*, on the other hand, represents
India as metaphor of something other than itself, as a certain
metaphysical posture that translates into an image of profound unreality. It thus becomes that archetypal novel of
modernity that co-opts the space reserved for India in the
western literary imagination, so that all subsequent novels on
the Indian theme appear secretly obsessed with the desire to
describe exactly what transpired in the Marabar Caves" (170).

Forster's approach is "perhaps even more fraught with violence" than the Orientalist mode which aimed at understanding the Other in order to hold sway over it. In refusing to
'other' it, India as illusory and intangible *becomes a passage*
back for the western mind. India as perpetual regression becomes the manifestation of the unconceivability of that mind.
Suleri reminds us that later narratives are impacted upon by
this prototype, so that India's difference is represented as a
cave bereft of any independent, uncontrolled meaning.

The failure to grapple with the otherness of India is transferred by the liberal imagination and projected onto its object,
India. A mapping of the "desire to convert unreadability into
unreality" (171) is enacted by the novel. The protagonists, in
being challenged by the 'unknowableness' of India, are quick
to attribute it to its space and its people, disallowing any possibility of a perceptual inadequacy in their vision. Thus, the
authorial voice in the novel: "The fissures in the Indian soil
are infinite: hinduism [*sic*], so solid from a distance, is riven

into sects and clans, which radiate and join, and change their names according to the aspect from which they are approached. Study it for years with the best teachers, and when you raise your head nothing they have told you quite fits" (Forster 1924/80: 289).

Soaked in the liberal discursive tradition, Forster appropriates the difference of India. Hinduism or Hindu spirituality is constituted as a danger to the West as the text, time and again, refers to India as a "muddle" whose "nihilism" appears to be destructive of western sensibility. The fate of Mrs Moore is a striking enactment of this menace. In contrast to Hinduism, Islam is not constituted as a metaphysical threat; Fielding's statement, which is reinforced with the general authorial stance, undermines it: "'There is no God but God', doesn't carry us far through the complexities of matter and spirit; it is only a game with words, really a religious pun, not a religious truth" (272). Alternatively, Hinduism is a lurking menace and cannot be undermined; it binds and coalesces with an emptiness which the western traveller must come to terms with spiritually. In this negotiation, it ceases to be the 'other'. This appropriation of Hinduism to serve the interests of the literary imagination is part of the liberal tradition of imperialism.

The movement from engagement with Indian metaphysics (which willy-nilly end up essentializing India) or Forster's narrative skills to issues of race and gender, is marked by its virtual non-existence in the Indian classroom. This state of affairs in the teaching of English literature is sustained by the complicity between classroom lectures, 'mainstream' literary criticism, and the ubiquitous *kunji* or Indian bazaar guide. The *kunji* is literally a key to examination success as it "gathers together all the acceptable critics and squeezes them into ready-prepared answers" providing "explicitly ... what ... dominant pedagogy demands". In this way it obviates "the need to go and read twenty unavailable books" (Loomba 1989: 79).

There are many such *kunjis* or cram-books available on Forster's *A Passage to India* and they are widely used by students in colleges and universities throughout the country. Leaving aside that form of 'indigenous' criticism, I want to consider a collection of critical essays which appeared with the avowed aim of providing an 'Indian response' to the reading of Forster's novel. Vasant Shahane, the editor, introduces the collection explaining its *raison d'etre* on the grounds that the western reception of the novel places undue stress on "the patterns of common heritages and parallelism in the theories of east and west" (1975: xiii).

Despite its editorial ambition, however, the collection offers only a more detailed meandering into the world of Indian philosophical meditations than what the western critics' discussions on the novel's spiritual dimension had provided so far. The critics' interpellation as colonized readers seems complete as they reproduce the same categories and strategies in their interpretative schema that go to make up orientalist discourse (see also Pathak and Sengupta 1991). And there is no space here for a Bhabhaesque dissension to be recovered. Theirs is a totally dehistoricized approach to a text that quite explicitly demands a political reading. One of the contributors, in fact, asserts that the novel's theme is not race relations. It is, he argues, about "fundamental experience" and is "symbolic of the contemporary situation". Spiritual alienation and "man's tragic predicament" has its Forsterian antidote in "[t]he Hindu concept of the absolute, that man is a part of the absolute and his chief goal is to unite with it ..." (34).

In the context of India, as I argue in my conclusion, it would be more enabling to insert English studies within the purview of a critical historical and cultural studies programme so that English culture, or the constitution of it, comes under scrutiny, rather than continue with the (well-established) ways of discovering how it "express[es] a reality" inaccessible by other means.

Notes

1 No figure could be put with any degree of accuracy as to the number of speakers of English in India. It is generally held that relatively only a few speak the language despite its dominant commercial role. Ashok Mitra expresses a widely held view when he claims that "at least forty million people speak or read some sort of English, a not inconsiderable number when you remember that close to three-fifths of the nation are without letters and cannot sign their name in any language" (1989: 19). According to the 1991 Census data on English, 0.55 per cent of households use it as either the first or the second language; 0.51 per cent use it as the second language and only 0.04 per cent use it as the first language. There are no figures for those who use it as a third language. Mary Zurbuchen reports that 40 million (21.62 per cent) receive instruction through the medium of English out of the total of 185 million students enrolled in educational institutions in India (1992: 48).

2 This sense of a crisis was felt as early as 1960 when Professor V.K. Gokak, in his presidential address at the All India English Teacher's Conference, spoke about researching in the discipline: "Our research degrees in English language and literature need some consideration. English literature has been an inter-continental subject of study and an over-tapped area for research, with the result that research students in our universities frequently spend years in preparing theses which are hardly anything more than a collection of available critical dicta and a contribution not to knowledge, but to a whole heap of typescripts piled up in a university library" (quoted in Sastry 1993: 68-69). This is echoed thirty years later in the address of Professor S. K. Desai at a session of the Indian Association for English Studies in 1990: "Then later some aspirants rush in where angels fear to tread and try to do research in the much-trodden paths of, say, Indian writing in English or after much persuasion of the teacher, in some over-discovered area in American or British literature – topics where it is easy to find a good deal of critical material … . In fact, English studies in India are, to say the least … in doldrums" (quoted in Sastry 1993: 71).

3 A recent report by Sreenivasan Jain (1994), in *The Times of India*, describes the move towards proposed changes in the University of Delhi syllabus.

4 Responding to the perceived 'crisis', the editors of a volume brought out by the British Council in India, *Provocations: the Teaching of English Literature in India*, offer pragmatic approaches to be used in the Indian classroom. They are opposed to the import of 'latest theories' from the West and fearful that these seek "to use English departments in order to get rid of English altogether" (Marathe et. al. 1993: 6).

5 Prometheus' gift of fire, "as a weapon of protest and a means of extending nationalism towards political independence ..." has been invoked to describe the status of English in apartheid South Africa by the critic Es'kia Mphahlele (1984: 90).

6 'Aryanism' has meant different things in different times and places. In nineteenth century India it referred to the golden age of Vedic times as well as other moments in history when the achievements of Indian culture were thought to have reached their zenith. The invention of a tradition of Aryan glory is largely due to the Indologists who were looking for the roots of European culture. The decay and debasement of this tradition in India could then serve to legitimate colonial rule. William Jones, to cite an instance, appoints himself to the task of recovering the lost splendour of this civilization; in 'A Hymn to Surya' (1786), he foregrounds the significance of his act of translation for this project:

> And if they (the gods) ask, "What mortal pours
> the strain?" ...
> Say: from the bosom of yon silver isle,
> "Where skies more softly smile,
> "He came; and, lisping our celestial tongue,
> "Though not from Brahma sprung,
> "Draws Orient knowledge from its fountains pure,
> "Through caves obstructed long, and paths too
> long obscure" (n.d.: 286).

(See also Thapar 1989; Mitter 1983). For other inflections of the term, see Martin Bernal's *The Black Athena* (1987).

7   Considered as the founder of modern Bengali poetry and drama, Madhusudan Dutt went on to produce the much-acclaimed epic poem *Megnadh-Badh Kavya* in Bengali (see Radice (1993) for a brief appraisal).

8   American Black writing is full of such examples. *Narrative of the Life of Frederick Douglass, An American Slave, Written by Himself* (1960) is one obvious instance where the moment of the full appropriation of the master's language by Frederick is also the moment of the attainment of freedom from slavery.

9   See Kumar (1991: 104-05). He cites Ellen E. McDonald and C.M. Stark, 'English Education, Nationalist Politics and Elite Groups in Maharashtra, 1885-1915', *Occasional Papers of the Centre for South and South East Asian Studies* (Berkeley 1969) as evidence.

10 Macaulay had prognosticated that "having become instructed in European knowledge, they may in some future age demand European institutions. Whether such a day will ever come I know not ... . Whenever it comes it will be the proudest day in English history" (quoted in Mishra 1961: 150). The English educated elite that was chiefly formed as result of Anglicist educational policies came to appeal to the political rhetoric of English liberalism to counteract Britain's imperialist praxis. The Universities Act of 1904 was largely a move designed to halt this liberal by-product of English education. The dissemination of liberal ideas was seen by Lord Curzon's time as a threat to the interests of empire.

The Indian National Congress thus became the *bete-noire* of Curzon: "My policy, ever since I came to India, has been to reduce the Congress to impotence" (quoted in Sarkar 1983: 105). For Gandhi, the connexion between the English language and the transfer of British liberalism is non-existent: "Of all the superstitions that affect India, none is so great as that a knowledge of English language is necessary for imbibing ideas of liberty, and developing accuracy of thought" (1958: 10).

11 As a link language it serves as a vehicle of communication between linguistically separated regional populations; it is also described as the language of the "intellectual makeup" of the intelligentsia (Rao 1938). As Rajan puts it, "a large slice of Indian life, and particularly

of its decision-making strata, continues to reason and act in English" (1965: 81).

12 The term 'critical modernist' is Bhikhu Parekh's, which he usefully employs to describe those nationalists who "accepted the Western *model* or goals of modernisation but preferred a distinct Indian path to it" (1995: 25).

13 Bhabha further quotes from Macaulay's essay on Warren Hastings to point to the dissonance and ambivalence at the origins of colonial authority. "It is probable that writing 15,000 miles from the place where their orders were to be carried into effect", the Directors of the East India Company, "never perceived the gross inconsistency of which they were guilty … . Now these instructions, *being interpreted*, mean simply, 'Be the father and the oppressor of the people, be just and unjust, moderate and rapacious'" (1994: 95).

14 The account here of the state may suggest that it is reified. The Indian state surely is not a singular thing, but I use it as a shorthand for all the organs that go to constitute it. See Byres (1994) for a summation of problems concerning the nature of the post-colonial Indian state.

15 The first 'official' debates about the place of English in post-independence India occurred in the Constituent Assembly where the question of a national language was deliberated from the 12th September to 14th September, 1949. The use of the English language in institutions of public life was the chief concern. The case of Hindi as the national language was strong but aroused suspicion in the minds of representatives from the South. A case was made for Hindusthani on the grounds of national integration; there was support even for Urdu. But the general acceptance was that none of the modern Indian languages was 'developed' enough yet to fulfil the needs of a society negotiating the scientific, technological, industrial, legal, and global facets of modernity. Nor could any of the Indian languages serve as a link language, it was thought, as translations from English generated confusion. One of the members, S.V. Krishnamoorthy Rao, pointed out: "for compensation we use the word 'prihar', Kaka Kalekar uses the word (Nuksanbhari), Sri Rahul Sankrityayan uses (Kshatipurti), Guptaji uses (Muavija), Sri

Sunderlal says (Yatjan) ..." (*Constituent Assembly Debates* 1949: 1336-37).

16 The 'dual system' provides, for one small group, an English medium public school education and, for the school-going majority, an education through the medium of a regional language with an indifferent smattering of English for a few years (see also Sheth 1995).

17 Thus, Caliban in *The Tempest* seizes his master Prospero's language so that like Chinua Achebe he can say, "I have been given the language and I intend to use it" (1964: 445). It becomes for him an instrument of subversion: "You taught me language, and my profit on't/ Is to know how to curse: the red plague rid you,/ For learning me your language" (*The Tempest*, Act I, Scene 2, Lines 364-66).

18 Jonathan Dollimore and Alan Sinfield define cultural materialism as "a combination of historical context, theoretical method, political commitment and textual analysis ... Historical context undermines the transcendent significance traditionally accorded to the literary text and allows us to recover its histories; theoretical method detaches the text from immanent criticism which seeks only to reproduce it in its own terms; socialist and feminist commitment confronts the conservative categories in which most criticism has hitherto been conducted; textual analysis locates the critique of traditional approaches where it cannot be ignored" (1994: vii).

19 Eagleton finds that in the Victorian period, 'English' was "among other things, a project designed to pacify and incorporate the proletariat, generate sympathetic solidarity between the social classes, and construct a national cultural heritage which might serve to undergird ruling-class hegemony in a period of social instability" (1984: 65).

20 Unconcerned with anything outside the metropolis, F.R. Leavis codified the parameters concerning what is to be included and excluded from the English literary canon. A text finds admission into the canon if it is marked by high moral standards as well as formal excellence. Apart from being "distinguished by a vital capacity for experience, a kind of reverent openness before life, and a marked moral intensity" such texts, according to Leavis, are "very original

technically" (1971: 17-18). Using strict elitist terms, he rules out of the canon anything that he imagines as "bogus, cheap, or vulgar" (22). His high moral seriousness accompanied by an almost religious incense-burning notion of literary texts has established itself as the norm and guide for constructing syllabi for over four decades since the publication of his *The Great Tradition* in 1948.

21 Among many others, William Cain (1984) has argued that deconstruction in its analytical project has not achieved anything beyond New Criticism. While New Criticism demonstrates the unity of the art object, deconstruction works to unpack and break open the totalised structure of a work.

22 This can be concluded from the compiled bibliography of the titles of articles published during the five years before 1989 (see *Indian Journal of English Studies* 1989).

23 Some universities at the postgraduate level do have a section on Anglo-Saxon literature but it is read in the same Leavisite light as other texts. Even when radical texts such as John Osborne's *Look Back in Anger* are introduced (as in the syllabus, for instance, of North Bengal University or Vidyasagar University) the emphasis is on the central protagonist Jimmy Porter's Hamlet-like rage and angst, rather than the socio-historical moment of a post-war, post-colonial disillusionment in Britain.

24 I will quote at length from the Preface of an Indian edition of Shakespeare's *Othello* dated 1928, which continues to inform the kind of pedagogical practice that Joshi refers to. Ram Gopal and P. R. Singarachari write: "About 40 years ago, I went to and stayed in England for over three years in connection with my study for the Bar. It was then my great good fortune to witness some – alas! only some of the plays of Shakespeare beautifully staged and acted by well-known actors ... The impression, their performances left on me, was deep and enduring. It made me pause in silent awe and wonder at the mighty mind of Shakespeare and all that is imparted or conveyed by his writings, – the instructive lessons and truths, the wit and wisdom, the varied experiences and sensations of man in different stages of his development, his instincts and emotions, in fact, the whole philosophy of human life, – in language quite

Shakespearean in its range, volume, variety, force and flexibility" (i). "A sight or study of Shakespeare's pictures of diversified human life makes us so familiar with them that they constantly and pertinaciously dwell in our imagination. In fact, they become to us more palpable, real, breathing, living figures than those of actual life. The latter touch and influence us while we are in contact with them; their sayings and doings dwell in our memory for a time only; but Shakespeare's characters have an ever-present, ever-lasting life, – almost as eternal as the human race." (i-ii). Once the universality of certain values is acknowledged or established the justification of Empire follows almost automatically. One of the most respected scholars of English in India who also helped to bring in American and Commonwealth Literature in Indian university syllabuses, C.D. Narasimhaiah, has this to say in a volume he edited about Shakespeare's coming to India: "the England of trade, commerce, imperialism and the penal code has not endured but the imperishable Empire of Shakespeare will always be with us. And that is something to be grateful for" (1964: v). See also note 4, Chapter One.

25 Thus, as the findings of the University Grants Commission report state: "Non-British Literature (e.g., American, Commonwealth, Indian, Comparative, European, etc.) are offered mostly as optional courses" (*Report* 1989: 21).

26 As Dharwadker (1993) argues: "[T]he literary orientalists concerned with India adopted an all-inclusive conception of literature, not because their Indian materials demanded or gave rise to it, but because it was the radical new conception that had begun transforming Europe's self-definition and self-understanding in their times. They also adopted such a conception because it enabled them to treat literature as complete (totalized, totalizable) expression of the "character," "spirit," or racial and cultural identity of a nation. Moreover, it allowed them to occupy the typical site of cross-cultural encounter within the institutional framework of colonialism, in which "literature" and its study defined the European self and the oriental other in the same discursive space, at the same moment" (167-68). See Martin Bernal's *The Black Athena* (1987) for the pur-

pose that the project of philology and, in particular, the study of
Sanskrit as the oldest of all Indo-European languages served to define an 'Aryan' identity.

27 Deploying a romantic conception of literature as 'expressive', 'me-
    diaeval' Indian literatures could be read in a restricted way. Thus the
    fate of the reformist *Bhakti* texts like those of Kabir in Hindi, Tu-
    karam in Marathi, Caitanya in Bengali, etc.

28 Susie Tharu gives the example of the Vaishnava singers to show a
    "selective *marginalization* and *delegitimation* of existing litera-
    tures and literary practices, and the constitution of a classical Indian
    literary tradition". The Vaishnava singers and dancers in nineteenth
    century Bengal were "hounded out of existence and their art de-
    nounced as the respectability of the middle class bhadramahila and
    the purity of her art was defined in counterpoint to the unbridled
    sexuality of the Vaishnava artists and the ribaldry of their songs
    and dances" (1991: 171; emphases in original).

29 Tejaswini Niranjana (1991) in her essay 'Translation, Colonialism
    and the Rise of English' relates the role of the orientalist William
    Jones and his efforts in translating ancient Indian legal and literary
    texts. This standardisation of a set of hegemonic colonial texts im-
    pressed linear historical narratives on Indians educated in English.

30 Chandu Menon's *Indulekha* (1887) and Nazir Ahmed's *Mirat ul
    Uroos* (1869), writes Tharu, reintroduce the good woman/bad
    woman subject of Hannah Catherine Mullen's *Phulmoni Karunar
    Bibaran* (1852) and other novels, but works which begin to subvert
    these oppositions also appear in the period.

31 The protagonist of R.K. Narayan's novel, *The English Teacher*,
    fumes against the modes of English teaching but reserves a high re-
    gard for its literature. "[A] whole century of false education" is eas-
    ily reconciled with "What fool could be insensible to Shakespeare's
    sonnets or the Ode to the West Wind or 'A Thing of Beauty is a joy
    for ever'" (1945: 220-21). The English book, as Viswanathan (1989)
    shows, remained dissociated from the actual material practices of
    imperialism. This acceptance of English literature as separate from
    its national enunciatory site has also made acceptable the 'universal'
    values embodied in it.

32 Apart from curriculum and evaluation committees which go on about it, the discourse focusing on issues of standards and quality is also produced in many journal articles which bemoan the 'decline' of English studies in India. A case in point is S. Nagarajan's 'The Decline of English in India: Some Historical Notes' (1981).

33 Apart from the dominant imperialist, nationalist, and Marxist historiographical accounts about the colonial period in India, a new movement has produced alternative readings of this period. Drawing from structuralist and poststructuralist critiques of the sovereign subject, this new movement in historiography has two vectors. The first is the highly acclaimed and influential group called the Subaltern Studies collective; and the second, what might be called 'Post-Orientalist' after Gyan Prakash's seminal essay 'Writing Post-Orientalist Histories of the Third World: Perspectives from Indian Historiography'. Both these schools challenge and rewrite imperialist as well as nationlist constructions of the colonial period in Indian history.

34 G.K. Das (1977) and Jeffrey Meyers (1973) also undertake similar readings of the novel. Molly Mahood (1977) relates the novel to the political upheavals of the 1920s.

Conclusion
'deigns to travel ...'

Even when Culture la Cultural Studies deigns to travel, its cara-
vansary has its preferred anglophile vacation spots. India def-
initely wins out over Syria ...

Lavie and Swedenburg 1996: 154

The status and function of the 'fiction' of English literature is
not natural but historically contingent. To demonstrate this
has been the burden of my book: from the reasons why English studies came to exist in India in the first place, to the
mythical value that it has lived by, and which is currently
under attack by various critics. Its contingent status is also
clear from the history of the discipline in England itself, as it
changed from a position of low standing in symbolic terms to
one so high that it became the keystone of the national curriculum in Britain (see Doyle 1982). "Once it had been established as part of a successful modern institution within higher education", writes Doyle, "English studies excluded from
its ambit those wider social processes through which fictions
are produced, circulated, and consumed. By legitimizing only
the study of 'valuable works', the discipline manufactured an
essential and unbridgeable distance between its own sphere of
high art and the general domain of popular fiction and discourse" (1989: 6).

This study of 'valuable works' has continued unabatedly in
a nationalist independent India. While the state struggles to
define the cultural and educational needs of the nation, in

texts such as the *Kothari Commission Report* and the *Haksar Commission Report*, it is still ambiguous about the role of English in the society at large. The questions relating to English studies which I am concerned with in this book have largely been unasked.

The investment in modernization that we encountered in the commission reports and *National Policy on Education* is resurrected in the neo-modernization theory of 'realistic' neo-liberal reform in India encouraged by the World Bank and the International Monetary Fund. But alongside this is also the emergence of resistance to modernity and development discourse (see Shiva 1988; Escobar 1987).

I have stressed the authoritative power of official discourse in fixing and closing the boundaries of social processes. But the ambivalence of authority at the heart of its enunciation has been theorized by Bhabha to indicate the possibilites of disruption and the negotiation that always occurs with the 'English Book' (1986a). This involves awareness of the political morality of every day life in Nandy's terms or the privileging of the "performative" over the "pedagogical", in Bhabha's terms, where "the people must be thought in a double-time":

The scraps, patches, and rags of daily life must be repeatedly turned into the signs of a national culture, while the very act of the narrative performance interpellates a growing circle of national subjects. In the production of the nation as narration there is a split between the continuist, accumulative temporality of the pedagogical, and the repetitious, recursive strategy of the performative. It is through this process of splitting that the conceptual ambivalence of modern society becomes the site of writing the nation …

The people are neither the beginning nor the end of the national narrative; they represent the cutting edge between the totalizing powers of the social and the forces that signify the more specific address to contentious, unequal interests and identities within the population". (1990: 297)

Knowledge has always been an integral part of development. What we need to emphasise is that it is a certain kind, a certain form of knowledge that is consecrated in the development regime. It has its roots in a certain epistemology. Issues relating to secularism and ecology in India are showing that modernity, western science, provide only one way, one path to knowledge; other epistemologies have existed and can exist.[1] Local struggles which redefine the relationship between humans, nature, and the economy of violence have global ramifications in their promise of transformation. "They are modest manifestations of a search, non-theorized and non-verbalized," Vandana Shiva says, "for an alternative scientific and technological culture, for an alternative development paradigm; an alternative concept of state and security; and, with their stress on non-violence and justice and peace, an alternative civilization" (1987: 257).

Traditions, perhaps, must give place to new traditions,[2] and that is perhaps where the value of hybridity (as opposed to the essentialist notions of organic culture, the confines of which are often seen to correspond with the borders of nations) begins to take on a political significance. It is an empowering notion in that hybridity is seen as "a *problematic* of colonial representation ... that reverses the effects of the colonialist disavowal, so that other 'denied' knowledges enter upon the dominant discourse and estrange the basis of its authority" (Bhabha 1985: 156; the model is discussed at length in the first chapter).

The heteroglossic hybridity of Bakhtin (that goes beyond just the dialogic speech situation and into the world where different 'languages' are constantly competing for hegemony) is opposed to the monoglossic discourses of colonial and national making. I am, of course referring here to the monoglossic texts of the KCR and NPE in particular. The recognition of cultural difference (as opposed to diversity) will take us beyond ethnocentricism or the construction of universal values. Local knowledge systems anticipate alternative political spaces (see Kothari 1987).

In that sense, India may well be considered as more post-modern (not as something coming *after*, but the 'post' signi-fying a condition that is counter to that which it qualifies) than 'modern'[3] (Dallmayr 1992). Nandy's formulations con-cerning the loss and recovery of the self under (post)colonial-ism seem useful in this moment of counter-modernity. "What looks like Westernization", he argues, "is often only a means of domesticating the West" (1983: 108). In his categorisation, the "players" are those who have sold out to the West, a sort of comprador class whose interests are with transnational cap-ital. The "counter-players" are those whose career takes on a path that involves critiquing the West whilst they partake of modernity. The Nehruvian project is a prime example of this as it opts "for a non-West which itself is a construction of the West". But the most enabling are the rare breed of "non-players" who (like Gandhi), under the powerful impetus of ac-culturation, nevertheless "construct a West which allows them to live with the alternative West, while resisting the loving embrace of the west's dominant self" (1983: xiv). Concepts, categories, defences of the mind are required for this kind of resistance to reduce "the West into a reasonably manageable vector within the traditional world views still outside the span of modern ideas of universalism. The first concept in such a set has to be the victims' construction of the West, a West which would make sense to the non-West in terms of the non-West's experience of suffering" (xiii). This has been the Gandhian project of *sarvodaya* but it still is bound in terms of the Other. Occidentalism of this nature tends to negate – at least under-emphasize – power mechanisms in discourse.

Forms of 'hybridity' and 'transgression' that are emerging from the margins (Bhabha 1994; Hall 1992, 1993a) disrupt and challenge the homogenizing and 'fixing' project of modernity and of nations as "engine[s] of modernity" (Hall 1992: 292). The problem of modernity is key to my attempt to describe an inclusive, participatory politics which can overcome the worst excesses of the metropolitan-indigenous binary. It depends very much on being able to isolate the structures of modernity – professional classes; parliaments; committees and their constitution; educational practice itself – and imagine a situation in which these things are transformed.

My book has focused on official discourses, both Indian nationalist and British. In order to extend this approach it would be necessary to look at 'vernacular' discourse (see Bodnar 1992), the agential sites of local resistance and negotiation with power as well as the non-resisting, reproducing and 'common-sensical' (in Gramsci's sense) constituencies. In my chapter on culture, I indicated how, by trying to guarantee a 'unity in diversity' and by promoting secularism, official discourses also define Indian culture as a distinct way of life. The modernity of such a perspective also separates out, museumifies and commodifies, the 'folk' cultures as was clearly evident in the touring exhibitions of 'folk' elements in the mosaic of Indian culture during the India festivals abroad and the 'Apna Utsav' in New Delhi.[4] Folk forms, as Williams reminds us, are seen as 'survivals', as continuing "by force of habit into a new state of society" (1976: 136-07). The implication is that these cultural practices – dances, songs, costumes – signify surviving forms of non-progressive traditions. 'Vernacular' discourses could provide a challenge to this perspective.

I am concerned here about the broad outline of a principle, rather than a particular curriculum development. By calling for a critical historical and cultural studies, I am not suggesting that it should become part of the already existing disciplinary rubric of 'area studies'. The history of area studies is closely allied to unequal power relations among nations (or geographical regions), especially the relation of the West to the rest. Thus, H.A.R. Gibb, Director of the Centre for Middle Eastern Studies, Harvard, in his book *Area Studies Reconsidered* (1964) uses the terms 'area studies' and 'oriental studies' interchangeably. He prescribes an 'interdisciplinary' approach with the objective of preparing students for careers in public life and business. Said rightly points out that 'modern Orientalists' or 'area experts' are indistinguishable from other experts of the policy sciences. Both of these groups are engaged in "the military-national-security possibilities of an alliance" (Said 1979: 197).

Not surprisingly, as nationalists occupying the homonymous space created by colonialism, area study formulators and scholars in India generally do not transcend the limitations of what Said has called 'new American Orientalism'. In fact, the recommendations made by the Experts Committee set up by the University Grants Commission in April 1963 "to consider a scheme for the development of area studies in Indian universities" (Appadorai 1987) betrays the fact that the concept of area studies is not much different from that in the West. The UGC guidelines issued to various area study centres dated January 5, 1982, stress that there should be a "close interaction between the academics in the programme and the administrative machinery of the Government of India". The latest circular dated September 23, 1987 is even more direct in its prescription: "The result of the studies in these centres should be useful in the formulation of our national policies in foreign affairs, defence, culture and in the spheres of bilateral, multilateral and regional co-operation ..." (quoted in Poddar and Subba 1992: 249).

Existing centre-periphery knowledge relations point to the need to address the neocolonial assumption which rejects the possibility of spaces in the 'East' as sources of knowledge.[5] That, again, as I stressed in the first chapter, is not to serve as an excuse for nativism, nostalgia and nationalism. Nor am I arguing for a kind of Occidentalism which will invert the procedures of Orientalism. Given the disbalance in global power relations, that project is already a non-starter.[6] Robert Young in dialogue with Gayatri Spivak sums up the difficulties of having a legitimate study project in his anecdote about an Indian friend visiting Britain on a British Council grant in order to research a book on post-structuralism in Britain:

It seemed to me too reverential a project. I said, why don't you write a book on the way poststructuralism has affected thinking in India, or, but this is perhaps in itself a neocolonial demand, investigate the extent to which Saussure, who [as] a Sanskrit scholar [...] developed many of his ideas on the sign, commonly presented as coming from nowhere, from Panini and Sanskrit semiotics. What bothered me about my friend's poststructuralist project was what I perhaps assumed too quickly to be a passive relation, repeating the colonial structure, that there is something in Britain called poststructuralism that is worth academics in India studying, and that seemed a clear case of theory working in a neocolonial way – similar to the way that Leavis' ideas were exported intact to Indian English departments". (1991: 234)

In the first chapter I highlighted the attempt in Bhabha and Spivak to negotiate their own location and imbrication in the theory they deploy. Spivak shows how the constitution of the academy itself brackets out the most serious global questions. Radical critiques which arise from it tend to be trapped in "terms set out by the constituted academy" (MacCabe in Spivak 1987: x). The macro-politics of imperialism and internal colonialism must therefore be juxtaposed with a reflective eye on the microphysics of power in academic relations.

My contention throughout the book has been that we must make use of theory as a tool-kit regardless of where it originates, so long as we are aware of its possible political implications. Thus, poststructuralist theory, wherever it is located, must engage with the central issue in cultural debates and postcolonial thinking concerning the interactions of the global and the local. In academic terms this is to insist that Indian studies and metropolitan studies be joined. In the metropolis, especially in the U.S., cultural studies makes interventions on issues of race, gender, and other forms of difference, but it tends to frame "its inquiries around study of Western geo-historical periods, Western culture (majority or minority) under Western capital, or Euro-US textual practices of literary and media productions" or around some favourite "anglophile vacation spots" (Lavie and Swedenburg 1996: 169). My argument is that it is not this kind of discipline we need to forge but one that will constantly problematize and re-locate the received notions of 'field' (research space) and 'home' (writing place), of bounded and impermeable sites and positionalities. The question of how to prevent the imperative to 'constantly problematise' research fields from becoming a research field in itself, i.e. the difficulty in which endless problematising turns into a problematic endlessness, is something beyond the scope of my effort here.

An historically self-critical programme would of course problematise issues of national identity and national culture in India as well as internationally. This would include insights developed from theories of regional cultural, and sub-cultural, clusters within Britain as well as European forms of culture and their relations.[7] The study of signifying practices – without the "almost exclusively significatory politics of cultural studies" (McGuigan 1996: 185) – would include texts from popular culture in order to demystify the repressive operations of power and disclose ideology in action.[8]

In the British context there are three main arguments for this shift. Firstly, the binary that separates an internal canon from an external popular culture can no longer be sustained. Secondly, there are cognitive reasons for studying popular culture, as Anthony Easthope sums it up: "Just as the ancient study of rhetoric refused to draw hard boundaries at the limits of what comprised rhetoric and as, similarly, modern linguistics takes the whole of language practice as its preview, so cultural studies must be prepared to consider every form of signifying practice as a valid object if it is to count as a serious discourse of knowledge" (1991: 6).[9] Finally, the political reason put forward by Raymond Williams (to counter the Leavisite dichotomy between culture and civilisation) is that the discourses of the common people are just as worthy of study as those of the educated elite.

A notion of culture that refuses to accept the official definition of the social but takes into account the experience of social marginality leads us beyond the idea of art objects and introduces a notion of the provisional production of meaning and value. This notion of cultural difference allows us to take cognizance of the emergence of "non-canonical cultural forms" (Bhabha 1992: 47). Bollywood films, popular songs, pavement art, etc., are just some of the myriad forms of popular culture which have a claim to be studied.[10] And it is not just texts as they appear or come to us for consumption that need to be studied but the whole process of production and distribution, such that the ideological operations of representation or the repressive procedures of power are demystified. A fascinating example of the kind of direction is R. Srivatsan's (1991) work on Bombay films, in which he analyses both the icon-building procedures and the political economy involved in the making of cinema hoardings which are in turn used to sell these films.

In this respect, culture, even as a 'verb' (see Street 1993), may sound like a colony of academic disciplines which employ disciplinary technologies to enforce the limits of discourse (Foucault 1977). Institutional conditions regulate practices and any discipline – however radical – remains subject to restriction. What is imperative is unceasingly to keep in view these and wider socio-economic conditions. The institutionalization of cultural studies in Britain constitutes "a moment of profound danger" (Hall 1992b: 285).[11] The university must go beyond the discourses of educational rationales (liberal humanism; service to the state; disciplinary research) that characterize it, but any agenda for disciplinary decomposition, particularly one that seeks an "incessant re-coding of diversified fields of value" (Spivak 1990a: 226) must always be accompanied by a doggedly persevering critique of the place one inhabits.

Notes

1 In other words, one is arguing that we play, as Paul Feyerabend phrases it, the "game of Reason": "An anarchist is like an undercover agent who plays the game of Reason in order to undercut the authority of Reason (Truth, Honesty, Justice, and so on)" (1975: 32-33).

2 See chapter three note no. 10 for a discussion on the nature of tradition that I find enabling.

3 The 'post' here serves a similar function as that in postcolonialism as theorized by Bhabha, when he says that it must not be seen to add *up* but to add *to* (1990).

4 That this form of exhibiting has a history mired in colonialism can be argued from Carol Breckenridge's demonstration that "[o]bjects from India were [...] used to construct an ecumene that went beyond national boundaries, though its cultural forms facilitated the reification of the nation-state. This is one of the cultural paradoxes of imperialism" (1989: 214).

5 For those who dismiss this as preposterous, I refer them, to give just one example, to the grammar of Panini who contributed considerably to the development of Saussure's semiotics. See Singh (1992) for the poststructuralist elements in Panini's study of the sign. Also Martin Bernal's main argument in his *Black Athena* points to the collective amnesia that has charaterised western civilisation in its total purging of its Afro-Asiatic roots. Sanskrit semiotics, as I suggested in the first chapter, is one area that English departments in India need to put on their research agenda.

6 But a very illuminating example of Occidentalism can be found in Millie Creighton's 'Imaging the Other in Japanese Advertising Campaigns' in Carrier 1995. Whether Japan's construction of the *gaijin* can politically qualify as Occidentalism is another matter. And Japan still the Orient?

7 Thus future research projects might want to uncover detailed histories of English cultural transactions in different parts of India as well as the other colonies. Some work has already been done in the area. Two theses that come to mind are David Johnson's *Reproduc-*

tion of the Shakespeare Industry in South Africa (1993) and Conor MaCarthy's *Failed Entities: Culture and Politics in Ireland 1969-91* (1996). Another direction would be a mapping of global, local, post-colonial, relations in the various cultural productions especially in the vernacular languages.

8   I have continued to use the notion of 'ideology' even though I prefer 'discourse'. As Foucault says: "By correcting itself, by rectifying its errors, by clarifying its formulations, discourse does not necessarily undo its relations with ideology" (1972: 186).

9   Adorno (1977) might possibly offer an interesting alternative to this *inclusive* program, insofar as he argues for the need to distinguish discursive practices as opposed to subordinating them all to a superior standpoint. One wouldn't necessarily arrive at knowledge, simply by making your category (e.g. linguistics) more and more inclusive: there is something predetermined about the Easthope argument insofar as knowledge is conceptualised as the end result of somebody collecting enough 'stuff'. For Adorno the category of knowledge itself would involve more complex mediations and negations than what Easthope would appear to suggest. In *Aesthetics and Politics*, Adorno talks about the class antinomy of bourgeois culture vis-à-vis change: "only if the dialectic of the lowest has the same value as the dialectic of the highest ... Both bear the stigmata of capitalism, both contain elements of change... Both are torn halves of an integral, to which, however, they do not add up ..." (1977: 123). What is interesting is Adorno's standpoint, which questions the additive principle as if one could simply restore what has been excluded from the canon. The place that Adorno thinks thought can get to via reflection on the social division of labour/class is a much more difficult one to name since it involves a degree of transformation in the conditions of knowing itself.

10 This is already happening as more and more academics from English departments have begun to engage with popular films. An instance is the great deal of interest shown in the controversial Mani Ratnam film *Roja*, which is a take on the idea of the Indian nation as it is imag(in)ed in a time which has seen the rise of Hindu fun-

damentalism. Among articles it has provoked are: Niranjana (1994); Bharucha (1994); Chakravarthy and Pandian (1994).

11 Tony Bennett, however, argues that "one of the overriding disadvantages of constituting the history of cultural studies in the form of a narrative of institutionalization, a move away from the margins to the centre, is that, as Derrida predicted it always will, the question of the location of the centre and the margin proves to be a constantly movable feast" (1996: 144).

Bibliography

MANUSCRIPT SOURCES

India Office Records: *L/PS/20/D8. Report on a Visit to Sikhim and the Thibetan Frontier in Oct., Nov. and Dec. 1873 by J. Ware Edgar.*
India Office Records: *MSS Eur D. 998/20. A.J. Hopkinson Collection entitled 'The Mongolian Fringe'. 1921-1951.*

GOVERNMENT REPORTS AND PUBLICATIONS

Annual Report (MHRD) (1991) Ministry of Human Resources Development, Government of India.
Annual Report (1985-86; 1990-91; 1991-92; 1992-93; 1993-94) Department of Culture, Ministry of Human Resources Development, Government of India.
Calcutta University Commission Report 1917-19 (1919). Calcutta: Office of Superintendent of Government Printing, India.
Census of India, 1991: Provisional Population Totals. New Delhi: Registrar General and Census Commissioner, India.
Committee for Review on National Policy on Education, 1986, Towards an Enlightened and Humane Society (1990). New Delhi: Ministry of Human Resource Development.
Constituent Assembly Debates: Official Reports (n.d.). New Delhi: Lok Sabha Secretariat.
Education Commission, 1964-66: Report – Education and National Development (1966). Delhi: Manager of Publications [Kothari Commission Report].
Fifth Report from the Select Committee on the Affairs of the East India Company (1812). Vol. 1.

National Culture Policy 1992 (A draft document) (1992). New Delhi: Department of Culture, Ministry of Human Resource Development, Government of India.

National Policy on Education 1986 (1986). New Delhi: Ministry of Human Resource Development, Department of Education.

National Policy on Education – 1986: Implementation Report (1988). New Delhi: Ministry of Human Resource Development, Government of India.

National Policy on Education, 1986 – Programme of Action (1986). New Delhi: Department of Education, Ministry of Human Resource Development Government of India.

National Policy on Education (NPE), 1986: Revised Policy Formulation (1992). New Delhi: Department of Education.

Parliamentary Debates (1813). Vol. 26. Great Britain.

Parliamentary Papers (1854). Vol. 47. Great Britain.

Parliamentary Papers (Reports from Committees): East India Company's Affairs (1831-32). Vol. IX. Great Britain.

Parliamentary Papers (Reports from Committees): East India Sixth Report (1852-53). Vol. 29. Great Britain.

Parliamentary Papers: Second Report from the Select Committee of the House of Lords, Together with the Minutes of Evidence (1852-53). Vol. 32. Great Britain.

Post-War Educational Development in India. Report by the Central Advisory Board of Education (1944). Prepared by John Sargent. Delhi: Bureau of Education.

Report of the CABE Committee on Policy (1992). New Delhi: Department of Education, Ministry of Human Resource Development, Government of India.

Report of the Curriculum Development Centre in English (1989). New Delhi: University Grants Commission.

Report of the High-Powered Committee Appointed to Review the Performance of the National Academies and the National School of Drama, Department of Culture (1990). Ministry of Human Resource Development, Government of India [Haksar Committee Report].

Report of the Study Group on Teaching of English (1971). New Delhi: Ministry of Education and Youth Services, Government of India.

Report on Vocational Education in India (Delhi, the Punjab and the United Provinces). With a Section on General Education and Administration (1937). Prepared by E.A. Abbott and S.H. Wood.

Second Five Year National Development Plan 1956-61 (1956). Planning Commission, Government of India.

Secondary Education Commission, 1952-53. Report (1953). Madras: Ministry of Education [Mudaliar Commission].

Selections from Educational Records. Compiled by H. Sharp, 1965 (reprint). Delhi: National Archives of India.

Selections from the Minutes and the Official Writings of the Honourable Monstuart Elphinstone, Governor of Bombay (1884). Ed. George W. Forrest. London.

Selections from the State Papers of the Governors-General of India. Lord Cornwallis (1914). Ed. G. Forrest. London.

The Study of English in India (1967). New Delhi: Ministry of Education, Government of India.

Third Five Year National Development Plan 1961-66 (1961). Planning Commission, Government of India.

BOOKS, ARTICLES, REVIEWS, DISSERTATIONS, & CONFERENCE PAPERS

Achebe, Chinua (1964) 'The English Language and the African Writers'. *Moderna Sprak* 58(4).

Adorno, Theodor (1977) 'Letters to Walter Benjamin'. In *Aesthetics and Politics.* Eds. E. Bloch et al. London: New Left Books.

Aggarwal, J.C. (1992) *Education Policy in India: Retrospect and Prospect.* Delhi: Shirpa Publications.

Ahmad, Aijaz (1987) 'Jameson's Rhetoric of Otherness and the National Allegory'. *Social Text* 17.

Ahmad, Aijaz (1992) *In Theory: Classes, Nations, Literatures.* London: Verso.

Aiyar, S.P. (1973) *Modernization of Traditional Society and Other Essays.* Delhi: Macmillan.

Althusser, Louis (1969) *For Marx*. Trans. Ben Brewster. London: Verso.

Althusser, Louis (1971) *Lenin and Philosophy and Other Essays*. Trans. Ben Brewster. London: New Left Books.

Althusser, Louis (1976) *Essays in Self-Criticism*. Trans. G. Lock. London: Verso.

Amin, Samir (1982) 'Crisis, Nationalism, and Socialism'. In *Dynamics of Global Crisis*. Eds. Samir Amin, Giovanni Arrighi, Andre Gunder Frank, and Immanuel Wallerstein. New York: Monthly Review Press.

Anderson, Benedict (1983) *Imagined Communities: Reflections on the Origin and Spread of Nationalism*. London:Verso.

Appadorai, A. (1987) 'International and Area Studies in India'. *International Studies* 24(2).

Appadurai, Arjun (1990) 'Disjuncture and Difference in the Global Cultural Economy'. *Public Culture* 2(2).

Appadurai, Arjun (1993). 'Number in the Colonial Imagination'. In *Orientalism and the Postcolonial Predicament*. Eds. C. Breckenridge and P. van der Veer. Philadelphia: University of Pennsylvania Press.

Apple, Michael (1985) *Education and Power*. London: Ark.

Arasteh, R. (1962) *Education and Social Awakening in Iran*. Leiden: E.J. Brill.

Arnold, Mathew (1965) 'The Function of Criticism at the Present Time'. In *Essays in English Literature*. Ed. F.W. Bateson. London: University of London Press.

Arnold, Mathew (1969) *Culture and Anarchy*. Ed. J. Dover Wilson. Cambridge: Cambridge University Press.

Asad, Talal (1979) 'Anthropology and the Analysis of Ideology'. *Man* 14.

Aspinall, A. (1931) *Cornwallis in Bengal: the Administration and Judicial Reforms of Lord Cornwallis in Bengal, together with Accounts of the Commercial Expansion of the East India Company, 1786-1793, and the Foundation of Penang, 1786-1793*. Manchester: Manchester University Press.

Azim, Firdous (1993) *The Colonial Rise of the Novel*. London: Routledge.

Bakhtin, Mikhail (1981) *The Dialogic Imagination*. Ed. Michael Holquist. Austin: Texas University Press.

Bakhtin, Mikhail (1984) *Problems of Dostoevsky's Poetics*. Ed. and trans. Caryl Emerson. Minneapolis: University of Minnesota Press.

Baldick, Chris (1983) *The Social Mission of English Criticism 1848-1932*. Oxford: Clarendon Press.

Bannerjee, Sumanta (1989) *The Parlour and the State: Elite and Popular Culture in Nineteenth Century Bengal*. Calcutta: Seagull Books.

Barthes, Roland (1973) *Mythologies*. St. Albans: Paladin.

Barthes, Roland (1977) 'Writers, Intellectuals, Teachers'. In *Image – Music – Text*. Trans. Stephen Heath. London: Fontana.

Basu, A.N. (ed.) (1952) *Indian Education in Parliamentary Papers. Part I*. Bombay: Asia.

Basu, D.D. (1950) *Commentary on the Constitution of India*. Vol. 5. Calcutta: S.C. Sarkar & Sons.

Basu, Tapan et al. (1993) *Khaki Shorts and Saffron Flags*. New Delhi: Orient Longman.

Bayly, C.A. (1988) *Indian Society and the Making of the British Empire. New Cambridge History of India Vol. II, Part 1*. Cambridge: Cambridge University Press.

Beiner, Ronald (1992) *What's the Matter with Liberalism?* Berkeley, California, London: University of California Press.

Bennett, Tony (1996) 'Out in the Open: Reflections on the History and Practice of Cultural Studies'. *Cultural Studies* 10(1).

Bernal (1987) *Black Athena: The Fabrication of Ancient Greece 1785-1985*. Vol. 1. London: Free Association Books.

Bhabha, Homi K. (1983) 'The Other Question – the Stereotype and Colonial Discourse'. *Screen* 24(6).

Bhabha, Homi K. (1984) 'Representation and the Colonial Text: A Critical Explanation of Some Forms of Mimeticism'. In *The Theory of Reading*. Ed. Frank Gloversmith. Brighton: Harvester.

Bhabha, Homi (1984a) 'Of Mimicry and Man: The Ambivalence of Colonial Discourse'. *October* 28.

Bhabha, Homi K. (1985) 'Sly Civility'. *October* 34.

Bhabha, Homi K. (1986) 'Remembering Fanon. Self, Psyche, and the Colonial Condition'. Foreword to *Black Skin, White Masks*. Trans. Charles Lam Markmann. London & Sydney: Pluto Press.

Bhabha, Homi (1986a) 'Signs Taken for Wonders: Questions of Ambivalence and Authority under a Tree outside Delhi, May 1817'. In *Race, Writing and Difference*. Ed. H.L. Gates, Jr. Chicago: Chicago University Press.

Bhabha, Homi K. (1988) 'The Commitment to Theory'. *New Formations* 5.

Bhabha, Homi K. (1989) 'Beyond Fundamentalism and Liberalism'. *New Statesman*, March 3.

Bhabha, Homi K. (1990) (Ed.) *Nation and Narration*. London and New York: Routledge.

Bhabha, Homi K. (1990a) 'Introduction: Narrating the Nation', *Nation and Narration*. Ed. Homi Bhabha. London and New York: Routledge.

Bhabha, Homi K. (1990b) 'Dissemination: Time, Narrative, and the Margins of the Modern Nation'. In *Nation and Narration*. Ed. Homi Bhabha. London and New York: Routledge.

Bhabha, Homi K. (1990c) Interview: 'The Third Space'. In *Identity, Community, Culture, Difference*. Ed. J. Rutherford. London: Lawrence and Wishart.

Bhabha, Homi K. (1992) 'Freedom's Basis in the Indeterminate'. *October* 62.

Bhabha, Homi K. (1994) *The Location of Culture*. London & New York: Routledge.

Bhabha, Homi K. (1995) 'Secularism as an Idea will Change'. Interview with Vasu Srinivasan and Prem Poddar. *The Hindu*, December 17.

Bharucha, R. (1994) 'On the Border of Facism: Manufacture of Consent in *Roja*'. *Economic and Political Weekly of India*, June 4.

Bhattacharya, Gargi (1991) 'Cultural Education in Britain: From the Newbolt Report to the National Curriculum'. *Oxford Literary Review* 13.

Bodnar, John E. (1992) *Remaking America: Public Memory, Commemoration and Patriotism in the Twentieth Century*. Princeton: Princeton University Press.

Bourdieu, Pierre (1977) *Outline of a Theory of Practice*. New York: Cambridge University Press.

Bové, Paul (1986) *Intellectuals in Power*. New York: Columbia University Press.

Bowen, H.V. (1991) *Revenue and Reform: the Indian Problem in British Politics 1757-73*. Cambridge: Cambridge University Press.

Bowles, Samuel and Herbert Gintis (1976) *Schooling in Capitalist America: Educational Reform and the Contradictions of Economic Life*. London: Routledge and Kegan Paul.

Bradley, A.C. (1905) *Shakespearean Tragedy*. New York: Macmillan.

Breckenridge, Carol A. (1989) 'The Aesthetics and Politics of Colonial Collecting: India at World Fairs'. *Society for Comparative Study of Society and History* 31.

Breckenridge, Carol A. and Peter Van der Veer (eds.) (1993) *Orientalism and the Postcolonial Predicament*. Philadelphia: University of Pennsylvania Press.

Brennan, Timothy (1989) *Salman Rushdie and the Third World*. London: Macmillan.

Burghart, Richard (1990) 'Ethnographers and their Local Counterparts in India'. In *Localizing Strategies: Regional Traditions of Ethnographic Writing*. Ed. Richard Fardon. Washington D.C.: Smithsonian Press.

Butalia, Pankaj (1994) 'Not Outlaw, But Outcast'. *Sunday*, December 4-10.

Byres, Terence J. (ed.) (1994) *The State and Development Planning in India*. Delhi: Oxford University Press.

Cain, W.E. (1984) *The Crisis in Criticism: Theory, Literature and Reform in English studies*. Baltimore: Johns Hopkins University Press.

Centre For Himalayan Studies 1978-1986: A Brief Sketch (1986). Rajarammohunpur: N.B. University.

Chakraborty, Dipesh (1992) 'Postcoloniality and the Artifice of History: Who Speaks for Indian Pasts?'. *Representations* 37.

Chakravarty, Kumaresh (1986) 'The Compelling Crisis and the New Education Policy'. *Social Scientist* 153-54.

Chakravarthy, V. and M.S.S. Pandian (1994) 'More on *Roja*'. *Economic and Political Weekly of India*, March 12.

Chandra, Bipan (1987-88) *India's Struggle for Independence*. New Delhi: Viking.

Chandra, Sudhir (1992) *The Oppressive Present: Literature and Social Consciousness in Colonial India*. Delhi: Oxford University Press.

Chatterjee, Partha (1986) *Nationalism and the Colonial World: A Derivative Discourse?*. London: Zed Books.

Chatterjee, Partha (1986a) 'Transferring a Political Theory'. *Economic and Political Weekly of India* 21(3).

Chatterjee, Partha (1990) 'A Response to Taylor's "Modes of Society"'. *Public Culture* 3(1).

Chatterjee, Partha (1994) *The Nation and its Fragments*. Princeton: Princeton University Press.

Chatterjee, T.K. (1986) 'The New Education Policy: A Class Necessity'. *Social Scientist* 153-154.

Chaube, S.K. (1985) *The Himalayas: Profiles of Modernization and Adaptation*. New Delhi: Sterling Publishers.

Chaudhuri, Nirad (1951) *The Autobiography of an Unknown Indian*. London: Macmillan.

Chow, Rey (1993) 'Ethics After Idealism'. *Diacritics* 23(1).

Clark, John (1912) *Aristotle's Poetics and Shakespeare's Tragedies*. Cape Town: Townshend, Taylor and Snashall.

Clokie, H.M. and J.W. Robinson (1937) *Royal Commissions of Inquiry: the Significance of Investigations in British Politics*. Stanford: Stanford University Press.

Cohn, B.S. (1985) 'The Command of Language and the Language of Command'. In *Subaltern Studies IV*. Ed. Ranajit Guha. Delhi: Oxford University Press.

Cohn, B.S. (1987) *An Anthropologist Among Historians and Other Essays*. Delhi: Oxford University Press.

Conroy, Martin (1974) *Education as Cultural Imperialism*. New York: David McKay.

Cory, W. (1882) *A Guide to Modern English History. Part II.* London: Kegan, Paul & French.

Creighton, Millie R. (1995) 'Imaging the Other in Japanese Advertising Campaigns'. In *Occidentalism: Images of the West.* Ed. James G. Carrier. Oxford: Clarendon Press.

Dale, Roger (1989) *The State and Education Policy.* Milton Keynes: Open University Press.

Dallmayr, Fred (1992) 'Modernisation and Postmodernisation: Whither India?'. *Alternatives* 17(4).

Das, G.K. (1977) *E.M. Forster's India.* London: Macmillan.

Das, Veena (1989) 'Difference and Divisions as Designs of Life'. In *Contemporary India: Essays on the Uses of Tradition.* Ed. Carla Borden. Delhi: Oxford University Press.

Das, Veena (1994) 'The Anthropological Discourse on India: Reason and its Other'. In *Assessing Cultural Anthropology.* Ed. Robert Borofsky. New York: McGraw-Hill.

Dasgupta, Probal (1993) *The Otherness of English: India's Auntie-Tongue Syndrome.* New Delhi: Sage.

Davis, Lance E. and Robert A. Huttenbach (1987) *Mammon and the Pursuit of Empire: The Political Economy of British Imperialism 1860-1912.* New York: Cambridge University Press.

de Certeau, M. (1984) *The Practice of Everyday Life.* Berkeley: University of California Press.

Defoe, Daniel (1927) *A Tour Thro' the Whole Island of Great Britain.* 2 Vols. Ed. G.D.H. Cole. London: Peter Davies.

Deleuze, Giles (1986) *Foucault.* Paris: Editions de Minuit.

Derrett, J. (1968) *Religion, Law and the State in India.* London: Faber & Faber.

Derrida, Jacques (1976) *Of Grammatology.* Trans. Gayatri Chakravorty Spivak. Baltimore: Johns Hopkins University Press.

Derrida, Jacques (1986) 'But, beyond ...'. *Critical Inquiry* 13(1).

Dewey, Clive (1972) 'Images of Village Community: A Study of Anglo-Indian Ideology'. *Modern Asian Studies* 6(3).

Dharmpal (1983) *The Beautiful Tree.* Delhi: Impex Biblia.

Dharwadker, Vinay (1993) 'Orientalism and the Study of Indian Literatures'. In *Orientalism and the Postcolonial Predicament:*

Perspectives on South Asia. Eds. C. Breckenridge and P. van der Veer. Philadelphia: University of Pennsylvania Press.

Dirks, Nicholas (1987) *The Hollow Crown: An Ethnohistory of an Indian Kingdom.* Cambridge: Cambridge University Press.

Dirks, Nicholas (1992) *Culture and Colonialism.* Ann Arbor: University of Michigan Press.

Dirks, Nicholas B. (1992a) 'Castes of Mind'. *Representations 37.*

Dirks, Nicholas (1993) 'Colonial Histories and Native Informants: Biography of an Archive'. In *Orientalism and the Postcolonial Predicament.* Eds. C. Breckenridge and P. van der Veer. Philadelphia: University of Pennsylvania Press.

Dirlik, Arif (1994) 'The Postcolonial Aura: Third World Criticism in the Age of Global Capitalism'. *Critical Inquiry 20.*

Dodd, P. (1986) 'Englishness and the National Culture'. In *Englishness: Politics and Culture 1880-1920.* Eds. R. Colls and P. Dodd. London: Croom Helm.

Dollimore, Jonathan and Alan Sinfield (Eds.) (1994) *Political Shakespeare: Essays in Cultural Materialism.* Manchester: Manchester University Press.

Doyle, Brian (1982) 'The Hidden History of English studies'. In *Re-Reading English.* Ed. Peter Widdowson. London: Methuen.

Doyle, Brian (1989) *English and Englishness.* London and New York: Routledge.

Duffet, W.E., A.R. Hicks and G.R. Parkin (1942) *India Today: The Background of Indian Nationalism.* New York: John Day.

Dumont, Louis (1970) '"The Village Community": From Munro to Maine'. In *Religion, Politics and History in India: Collected Papers in Indian Sociology.* Paris: Mouton.

Eagleton, Terry (1983) *Literary Theory: An Introduction.* Oxford: Blackwell.

Eagleton, Terry (1984) *The Function of Criticism: from the The Spectator to Post-Structuralism.* London: Verso.

Eagleton, Terry (1991) *Ideology: An Introduction.* London: Verso.

Easthope, Antony (1991) *Literary Into Cultural Studies.* London and New York: Routledge.

Eliot, T.S. (1948) *Notes Toward a Definition of Culture*. London: Faber and Faber.

English M.A. Exam (Part I & II) 1989, 1990, 1991. University of North Bengal.

English – T.Y.B.A. Exam 1994. University of Bombay.

Escobar, Arturo (1984-85) 'Discourse in Development: Michel Foucault and the Relevance of his Work to the Third World'. *Alternatives* X(3).

Escobar, Arturo (1987) 'Power and Visibility: The Invention and Management of Development in the Third World'. Unpublished Ph.D. dissertation.

Fairclough, Norman (1992) *Discourse and Social Change*. Cambridge: Polity Press.

Fanon, Frantz (1967) *The Wretched of the Earth*. Harmondsworth: Penguin.

Fanon, Frantz (1986) *Black Skin White Masks*. London: Pluto Press.

Farquhar, J.N. (1967) *Modern Religious Movements in India*. New Delhi: Munshiram Munoharlal

Farrar, F.W. (ed.) (1867) (reprint 1969) *Essays on a Liberal Education*. London: Gregg.

Featherstone, Mike (ed.) (1990) *Global Culture*. London, Newbury Park, New Delhi: Sage.

Ferrer, Daniel (1990) *Virginia Woolf and the Madness of Language*. Trans. Geoffrey Bennington and Rachel Bowlby. London: Routledge.

Feyerabend, Paul (1975) *Against Method*. London: Verso.

Fishman, J. (1968) 'Nationality-Nationalism and Nation-Nationism'. In *Language Problems of Developing Nations*. Eds. J. Fishman, C. Ferguson and J. Das Gupta. New York: Wiley.

Forster, E.M. (1924/1980) *A Passage to India*. Hammondsworth: Penguin.

Foucault, Michel (1972) *The Archaeology of Knowledge*. London: Tavistock Publications.

Foucault, Michel (1977) *Discipline and Punish*. Harmondsworth: Penguin.

Foucault, M. (1980) *Power-Knowledge*. Ed. Colin Gordon. London: Harvester.

Foucault, M. (1981) 'The Order of Discourse'. In *Untying the Text: A Post-Structuralist Reader*. Ed. and intro. by Robert Young. Boston, London & Henley: Routledge, Kegan & Paul.

Foucault, Michel (1985) *The Use Of Pleasure*. New York: Vintage Books.

Freitag, Sandra B. (1989) *Collective Action and Community: Public Arenas and the Emergence of Communalism in North India*. Berkeley and Los Angeles: University of California Press.

Gadamer, H.G. (1982) *Truth and Method*. Trans. G. Barden and J. Cumming. New York: Crossroad.

Gallie, W.B. (1955-56) 'Essentially Contested Concepts'. *Proceedings of the Aristotlean Society* 56.

Gandhi, M.K. (1938) *Hind Swaraj*. Ahmedabad: Navajivan Press.

Gandhi, M.K. (1958) 'An Unmitigated Evil'. In *Evil Wrought by the English Medium*. Ed. K.N. Prabhu. Ahmedabad: Navajivan Printing House.

Gandhi, M.K. (1958-) *The Collected Works of Mahatma Gandhi*. Vol. 85. New Delhi: Publication Division.

Gandhi, M.K. (1962) *The Problem of Education*. Ahmedabad: Navajivan Press.

Garu, L.K.P. (1866) *The Social Status of the Hindus*. Benares.

Gates, Henry Louis Jr. (1991) 'Critical Fanonism'. *Critical Inquiry* 17.

Gellner, Ernest (1983) *Nations and Nationalism*. Oxford: Basil Blackwell.

Ghosh, Sankar (1974) *The Naxalite Movement: A Maoist Experiment*. Calcutta: Firma K.L.M.

Gibb, H.A.R. (1964) *Area Studies Reconsidered*. London: School of Oriental and African Studies.

Giddens, Anthony (1976) *New Rules of Sociological Method*. London: Hutchinson.

Gilroy, Paul (1987) *There Ain't No Black in the Union Jack*. London: Hutchinson.

Giroux, Henry (1982) *Theory and Resistance in Education*. South Hadley: Bergin and Garvey Publishers.

Gokak, V.K. (1963) 'Speech at the Plenary Session'. In *The Teaching of English Literature Overseas*. Ed. John Press. London: Methuen.

Goldberg, David Theo (1993) *Racist Cultures: Philosophy and the Politics of Meaning*. Oxford: Blackwell Publishers.

Gopal, Ram and P.R. Singarachari (eds.) (1928) *Shakespeare: Othello*. Bangalore: Bright and Company.

Graff, Gerald (1987) *Professing Literature: An Institutional History*. Chicago: Chicago University Press.

Gramsci, Antonio (1971) *Selections from Prison Notebooks*. Eds. and trans. Quinten Hoare and Geoffrey Smith. New York: International Publishers.

Grant, Charles (1797) *Observations on the State of Society among the Asiatic Subjects of Great Britain, particularly with respect to Morals; and on the means of Improving it*. London: privately printed.

Gray, John (1977) 'On the Contestability of Social and Political Concepts'. *Political Theory* 5(3).

Guha, Ranajit (1982) 'On Some aspects of the Historiography of Colonial India'. In *Subaltern Studies I: Writings on South Asian History and Society*. Ed. Ranajit Guha. Delhi: Oxford University Press.

Guha, Ranajit (1989) 'Dominance without Hegemony' and its Historiography'. In *Subaltern Studies VI*. Ed. Ranajit Guha. Delhi: Oxford University Press.

Guha, Ranajit (1992) 'Discipline and Mobilize'. In *Subaltern Studies VII*. Eds. Partha Chatterjee and Gyanendra Pandey. Delhi: Oxford University Press.

Guhan, S. (1985) 'Towards a Policy for Analysis'. In *Public Policy and Policy Analysis in India*. Eds. R.S. Ganapathy et al. New Delhi: Sage.

Gupta, Kshetra (1963) *Kabi Madhusudan o tār Patrabali*. Calcutta.

Hales, J.W. (1867) 'The Teaching of English'. In *Essays on a Liberal Education*. Ed. F.W. Farrar. London: Gregg.

Hall, Stuart (1980) 'Popular-democratic vs. authoritarian populism: two ways of taking democracy seriously'. In *Marxism and Democracy*. Ed. A. Hunt. London: Lawrence and Wishhart.

Hall, Stuart (1981) 'Notes on Deconstructing "the Popular"'. In *People's History and Socialist Theory*. London: Routledge.

Hall, Stuart (1992) 'The Question of Cultural Identity'. In *Modernity and its Futures*. Eds. Stuart Hall, David Held and Tony McGrew. Cambridge: Polity Press in association with Open University.

Hall, Stuart (1992a) 'The West and the Rest: Discourse and Power'. In *Formations of Modernity*. Eds. S. Hall and Bram Gieben. Cambridge: Polity Press in association with Open University.

Hall, Stuart (1992b) 'Cultural Studies and its Theoretical Legacies'. In *Cultural Studies*. Eds. Lawrence Grossberg, Paula Treichler and Cary Nelson. New York and London: Routledge.

Hall, Stuart (1993) 'The Local and the Global: Globalization and Ethnicity'. In *Culture, Globalization and the World System*. Ed. Anthony D. King. Binghampton: Macmillan in association with State University of New York.

Hall, Stuart (1993a) *'Old and New Identities, Old and New Ethnicities'*. In *Culture, Globalization and the World System*. Ed. Anthony D. King. Binghampton: Macmillan in association with State University of New York.

Hall, Stuart (1996) 'When was "the Postcolonial"? Thinking at the Limit'. In *The Post-Colonial Question: Common Skies, Divided Horizons*. Eds. Iain Chambers and Lidia Curti. London and New York: Routledge.

Harrison, David (1988) *The Sociology of Modernization and Development*. London: Unwin Hyman.

Hasan, Mushirul (1988) 'In Search of Integration and Identity: Indian Muslims since Independence'. *Economic and Political Weekly of India*. Special No. XXIII.

Hastings, Warren (1841) *Memoirs of the life of The Right Hon. Warren Hastings*. Ed. G.R. Gleig. London: Richard Bentley.

Hegel, G.W.F. (1956) *The Philosophy of History*. New York: Dover Publication.

Heimsath, Charles (1969) *Indian Nationalism and Hindu Social Reform*. Berkeley & Los Angeles.

Hill, Clifford and Kate Parry (eds.) (1994) *From Testing to Assessment: English as an International Language*. London and New York: Longman.

Himalayan Observer (1982) 16 (23).

Hobsbawm, Eric (1987) *The Age of Empire 1875-1914*. London: Weidenfeld & Nicolson.

Hobsbawm, Eric and Terence Ranger (eds.) (1983) *The Invention of Tradition*. Cambridge: Cambridge University Press.

Hogwood, B.W. and B. Guy Peters (1983) *Policy Dynamics*. Brighton: Wheatsheaf Books.

Hunter, Ian (1987) 'Review of *Marxism and Literary History*' by John Frow. *Southern Review* 20.

Hutchins, Francis G. (1967) *The Illusion of Permanence*. Princeton: Princeton University Press.

IJES Bibliography 1989 (1989) *Indian Journal of English Studies* XXVIII.

Illich, Ivan (1971) *De-schooling Society*. London: Calder and Boyars.

Inden, Ronald B. (1990) *Imagining India*. Oxford and Cambridge, Mass.: Basil Backwell.

Jain, Jasbir (1989) 'A Deconstructionist Reading of Moonstone'. *Rajasthan University Studies in English* 1.

Jain, Sreenivasan (1994) 'English Syllabus to be Liberated from Time Warp'. *The Times of India*', December 9.

Jameson, Frederick (1986) 'Third World Literature in the Era of Multinational Capitalism'. *Social Text* 15.

Jha, Amarnath (1941) 'Presidential Address'. All India English Teachers Conference.

Johnson, David (1993) 'Aspects of a Liberal Education: Late Nineteenth Century Attitudes to Race, from Cambridge to the Cape Colony'. *History Workshop Journal* 36.

Johnson, David (1993a) 'Reproduction of the Shakespeare Industry in South Africa'. D.Phil. Dissertation: Sussex University.

Johnson, Paul (1993) 'Colonialism is Back – and not a Moment Too Soon'. *The New York Times*, April 18.

Johnson, Richard (1977) 'Educating the Educators: "Experts" and the State 1833-9'. In *Social Control in Nineteenth Century Britain*. Ed. A.P. Donajgrodzki. London: Croom Helm.

Jones, William (n.d.) *Translations from Oriental Languages II*. Delhi: Pravesh Publications.

Jones, William (1786) 'On the Hindus'. In *The British Discovery of Hinduism in the Eighteenth Century* (1970). Ed. Peter J. Marshall. Cambridge: Cambridge University Press.

Joshi, Svati (1991) 'Rethinking English: An Introduction'. In *Rethinking English: Essays in Literature, Language, History*. Ed. Svati Joshi. New Delhi: Trianka.

Kachru, Braj (1989) 'Indian English'. *Seminar* 359.

Kant, Immanuel (1960) *Education*. Michigan: University of Michigan Press.

Kapur, G. (1988) 'Contemporary Cultural Practice: Some Polemical Categories', Paper presented at the Alam Khudmiri Memorial Lectures at Hyderabad.

Kaul, Suvir (1992) 'The Indian Academic's Resistance To Theory'. In *The Lie of the Land*. Ed. Rajeswari Sunder Rajan. Oxford University Press: New Delhi.

Kaviraj, Sudipto (1990) 'Capitalism and the Cultural Process' *Journal of Arts and Ideas* XIX.

Kaviraj, Sudipto (1991) 'On State, Society and Discourse in India'. In *Rethinking Third World Politics*. Ed. James Manor. London and New York: Longman.

Kaviraj, Sudipto (1995) *The Unhappy Consciousness, Bankimchandra Chattopadhyay and the Formation of Nationalist Discourse in India*. Bombay: Oxford University Press.

King, Anthony D. (ed.) (1993) *Cultural Globalization and the World-System*. Binghamton: State University of New York.

Kipling, R. (1994) *Kim*. Ed. Trever Royle. London: Everyman.

Kopf, David (1969) *British Orientalism and the Bengal Renaissance*. Berkeley & Los Angeles: University of California Press.

Kopf, David (1980) 'Hermeneutics Versus History'. *Journal of South Asian Studies* XXIX(3).

Kortenaar, Neil Ten (1995) '"Midnight's Children" and the Allegory of History'. *ARIEL* 26(2).

Kothari, Rajani (1987) 'On Humane Governance'. *Alternatives* XII(3).

Kumar, Krishna (1991) *Political Agenda of Education: A Study of Colonialist and Nationalist Ideas*. New Delhi: Sage Publications.

Kumar, Krishna (1992) 'Continued Text'. *Seminar* 400.

Laclau, Ernesto (1971) 'Federalism and Capitalism in Latin America' *New Left Review* 67.

Lavie, Smadar and Ted Swedenburg (1996) 'Between and Among the Boundaries of Culture: Bridging Text and Lived Experience in the Third World'. *Cultural Studies* 10(1).

Leavis, F.R. (1971) *The Great Tradition*. Harmondsworth: Penguin.

Lentricchia, Frank and Thomas McLaughlin (eds.) (1990) *Critical Terms for Literary Study*. Chicago: University of Chicago Press.

Liddle, A.V. (1990) 'The Role of Locals in Border Management'. In *India's Borders: Ecology and Security Perspectives*. Eds. Ramakrishna Rao and R.C. Sharma. New Delhi: Scholars Publishing Forum.

Loomba, Ania (1989) *Gender, Race, Renaissance Drama*. Manchester: Manchester University Press.

Loomba, Ania (1991) 'Overworlding the Third World'. *Oxford Literary Review* 13.

Loomba, Ania (1992) 'Criticism and Pedagogy in the Indian Classroom'. In *The Lie of the Land*. Ed. Rajeswari Sunder Rajan. Delhi: Oxford University Press.

Ludden, David (1993) 'Orientalist Empiricism: Transformations of Colonial Knowledge'. In *Orientalism and the Postcolonial Predicament*. Eds. C. Breckenridge and P. van der Veer. Philadelphia: University of Pennsylvania Press.

Lughod, Abu Janet (1993) 'Going Beyond Global Babble'. In *Culture, Globalization and the World System*. Ed. Anthony D. King. Binghamton: State University of New York.

Luke, A. (1994) 'Genres of Power? Literacy Education and the Production of Capital'. In *Literacy in Society*. Eds. R. Hasan and G. Williams. London: Longman.

Lukmani, Yasmeen (1972) 'Motivation to Learn and Language Proficiency'. *Language Learning* 22(2).

Lukmani, Yasmeen (1992) 'Attitudinal Orientation Towards Studying English Literature in India'. In *The Lie of the Land: English Literary Studies in India*. Ed. Rajeswari Sunder Rajan. New Delhi: Oxford University Press.

MaCarthy, Conor (1996) 'Failed Entities: Culture and Politics in Ireland 1969-91'. D.Phil. Dissertation: University of Sussex.

Macaulay, T.B. (1952) *Selected Speeches*. London: Oxford University Press.

MacCabe, C. (1985) 'English literature in a global context'. In *English in the World: Teaching and learning the language and literature*. Eds. Randolph Quirk and H.G. Widdowson. Cambridge: Cambridge University Press.

MacKenzie, John M. (1995) *Orientalism: History, Theory and the Arts*. Manchester: Manchester University Press.

Maclure, Stuart J. (1965) *Educational Documents. England and Wales 1816-1963*. London: Capman and Hall.

Maddox, Bryan (1995) 'Literacy as Sign'. B.A. Dissertation: University of Sussex.

Majeed, Javed (1992) *Ungoverned Imaginings: James Mill's The History of British India and Orientalism*. Oxford: Clarendon Press.

Mahood, Molly (1977) *The Colonial Encounter: A Reading of Six Novels*. London: Rex Collings.

Manchanda, Rita (1986) 'Culture: The Great Leap Forward'. *The Illustrated Weekly of India*, November 9.

Mani, Lata (1984) 'The Production of an Official Discourse on Sati in Early Nineteenth Century Bengal'. In *Europe and its Others*. Ed. Francis Barker. Colchester: University of Essex.

Marathe, S., M. Ramanan and R. Bellarmine (1993) *Provocations: the Teaching of English Literature in India*. Madras: Orient Longman in association with the British Council.

Marshall, P.J. (ed.) (1970) *The British Discovery of Hinduism in the Eighteenth Century*. Cambridge: Cambridge University Press.

Marx, K. & F. Engels (1959) *On Colonialism*. Moscow: Progress Publishers.

Mayhew, Arthur (1926) *The Education of India*. London: Faber.

Mazumdar, R.C. (ed.) (1965) *British Paramountcy and Indian Renaissance*. Vol. X, Part 2. Bombay: Bharatiya Vidya Bhavan.

McClintock, Anne (1994) 'The Angel of Progress: Pitfalls of the Term 'Post-colonialism''. In *Colonial Discourse and Post-colonial Theory: A Reader*. Eds. Patrick Williams and Laura Chrisman. Hertfordshire: Harvester Wheatsheaf.

McGuigan, Jim (1996) 'Cultural Policy Studies: Or, How to be Useful *and* Critical' *Cultural Studies* (10)1.

Memoirs of the Life of Right Honourable Warren Hastings, Vol I. (1841). Compiled by G.K. Gleig. London: Richard Bentley.

Metcalf, Thomas R. (1994) *Ideologies of the Raj: The New Cambridge History of India.* Cambridge: Cambridge University Press.

Meyers, Jeffrey (1973) *Fiction and the Colonial Experience.* New Jersey: Rowman and Littlefield.

Michael, Ian (1987) *The Teaching of English from the Sixteenth Century to 1870.* Cambridge: Cambridge University Press.

Mill, J.S. (1947) *On Liberty.* Ed. Albury Castell, New York: Appleton-Century-Crofts.

Mill, J.S. (1962) 'The Spirit of the Age'. In *Essays on Politics and Culture.* Ed. Gertrude Himmelfarb. New York: Peter Smith.

Mishra, B.B. (1961) *The Indian Middle Classes: Their Growth in Modern Times.* Bombay: Oxford University Press.

Mitchell, W.J.T. (1989) *The Chronicle of Higher Education,* April 19.

Mitra, Ashok (1989) 'The Empire is Dead. Long Live the Imperial Lingo'. *New Internationalist* 191.

Mitter, Partha (1977) *Much Maligned Monsters: A History of European Reactions to Indian Art.* Chicago and London: University of Chicago Press.

Mitter, Partha (1983) 'The Aryan Myth and British Writings on Indian Art and Culture'. In *Literature and Imperialism.* Ed. B. Moore-Gilbert. Roehampton: Roehampton Institute of Higher Education.

Mitter, Partha (1994) *Art and Nationalism in Colonial India 1850-1922.* Cambridge: Cambridge University Press.

Mitter, Partha (1995) 'Close Encounters with Far Pavilions'. Review of John MacKenzie's *Orientalism: History, Theory and the Arts. The Times Higher Education Supplement,* November 24.

Mohanty, Chandra (1988) 'Under Western Eyes: Feminist Scholarship and Colonial Discourse'. *Feminist Review* 30.

Moorhouse, Geoffrey (1983) *Calcutta: the City Revealed.* Harmondsworth: Penguin.

Morris, J. (1979) *Pax Britannica: the Climax of an Empire.* Harmondsworth: Penguin.

Mphahlale, Es'kia (1984) 'Prometheus in Chains: The Fate of English in South Africa'. *English Academy Review* 2.

Musselwhite, David (1986) 'The Trial of Warren Hastings'. In *Literature, Politics and Theory*. Eds. Francis Barker et al. London: Methuen.

Nagarajan, S. (1981) 'The Decline of English in India: Some Historical Notes'. *College English* 43(7).

Naik, J.P. (1965) *Educational Planning in India*. Bombay: Allied Publishers.

Naik, J.P. (1975) *Education, Quality and Quantity: The Elusive Triangle in Indian Education*. Bombay: Allied Publishers.

Naik, J.P. (1978) *Policy and Performance in Indian Education (1947-1974)*. New Delhi: Orient Longman.

Naik, J.P. (1982) *The Education Commission and After*. New Delhi: Allied Publishers.

Naipaul, V.S. (1977) *India: A Wounded Civilization*. Harmondsworth: Penguin.

Nandy, Ashis (1983) *The Intimate Enemy: The Loss and Recovery of Self Under Colonialism*. Delhi: Oxford University Press.

Nandy, Ashis (1987) *Traditions, Tyranny and Utopia*. New Delhi: Oxford University Press.

Nandy, Ashis (1988) 'Culture, State and the Rediscovery of Indian Politics', *Interculture* XXI(2).

Narasimhaiah, C.D. (1964) (ed.) *Shakespeare Came to India*. Bombay: Popular Prakashan.

Narasimhaiah, C.D. (1966) *The Swan and the Eagle*. Simla: Indian Institute of Advanced Study.

Narasimhaiah, C.D. (1993) 'Retrospect and Prospect'. In *Provocations*. Eds. Sudhakar Marathe et al. Madras: Orient Longman.

Narayan, R.K. (1945) *The English Teacher*. London: Eyre and Spottiswoode.

Nehru, J.L. (1974) *The Discovery of India*. Bombay: Asia.

Ngugi, Thiong wa (1972) 'On the Abolition of the English Department'. In *Homecoming: Essays on African and Caribbean Literature, Culture and Politics*. London: Heinemann.

Niranjana, Tejaswini (1991) 'Translation, Colonialism and the Rise of English'. In *Rethinking English: Essays in Literature, Language, History*. Ed. Svati Joshi. New Delhi: Trianka.

Niranjana, Tejaswini (1994) 'Integrating Whose Nation? Tourists and Terrorists in *Roja*'. *Economic and Political Weekly of India*, January 15.

Nirvendananda, Swami (ed.) (1976) *Swami Vivekanada on India and her Problems*. Calcutta: Advaita Ashrama.

Norbu, Dawa (1992) *Culture and Politics of Third World Nationalism*. London: Routledge.

Outram, Steve (1989) *Social Policy*. Essex: Longman.

Ovens, David (1968) 'Investment in Human Capital'. In *The Crisis of Indian Planning in the 1960s*. Eds. P. Streeten and M. Lipton. London: Oxford University Press.

Owen, S.J. (ed.) (1800) *A Selection from the Despatches Relating to India of the Duke of Wellington*. London.

Panchmukhi, P.R. (1978) *Educational Reform in India: A Century of Effort*. Washington D.C.: World Bank Publication No. 671-19.

Pandey, Gyan (1990) *The Construction of Communal Consciousness in Colonial India*. Delhi: Oxford University Press.

Pannikar, K.N. (1985) 'The Intellectual History of Colonial India: Some Historiographical and Conceptual Questions'. In *Situating Indian History*. Eds. S. Bhattacharya and Romila Thapar. Delhi: Oxford University Press.

Pannikar, K.N. (1987) 'Culture and Ideology: Contradictions in Intellectual Transformation of Colonial Society in India'. *Economic and Political Weekly of India*, December 5.

Paranjape, Makarand R. (1989) 'The Invasion of "Theory": An Indian Response'. *The Indian Journal of English studies* XXVIII.

Parekh, Bhikhu (1995) 'Jawaharlal Nehru and the Crisis of Modernisation'. In *Crisis and Change in Modern India*. Eds. Upendra Baxi and Bhikhu Parekh. New Delhi: Sage.

Parry, Benita (1985) 'The Politics of Representation in *A Passage to India*'. In *A Passage to India: Essays in Interpretation*. Ed. John Beer. London: Macmillan.

Parry, Benita (1987) 'Problems in Current Theories of Colonial Discourse'. *Oxford Literary Review* 9.

Parsons, T. (1971) *A System of Modern Societies*. Englewood Cliffs, NJ: Prentice-Hall.

Pathak, Z. and S. Sengupta (1991) 'The Prisonhouse of Orientalism'. *Textual Practice* 5(2).

Patra, A.N. (1987) *Committees and Commissions on Indian Education 1947-1977: A Bibliography*. New Delhi: National Council of Educational Research and Training.

Poddar, P.K. and T.B. Subba (1992) 'Unpacking Home-Grown Orientalism and Area Studies in India'. *Journal of Indian Anthropological Society* 27.

Pollock, Sheldon (1993) 'Deep Orientalism: Notes on Sanskrit and Power Beyond the Raj'. In *Orientalism and the Postcolonial Predicament*. Eds. C. Breckenridge and P. van der Veer. Philadelphia: University of Pennsylvania Press.

Prakash, Gyan (1990) 'Writing Post-Orientalist Histories of the Third World: Perspectives from Indian Historiography'. *Comparative Studies in Society and History* 32.

Radhakrishnan, R. (1987) 'Ethnic Identity Post-Structuralist Différance'. *Cultural Critique* 7.

Radice, William (1993) 'Milton and Madhusudan'. In *Institutions and Ideologies*. Eds. Peter Robb and David Arnold. Surrey: Curzon Press.

Rai, Amrit S. (1993) 'A Lying Virtue: Ruskin, Gandhi and the Simplicity of Use Value'. *South Asia Research* 13(2).

Rai, Lajpat (1966) *The Problem of National Education in India*. New Delhi: Publications Division.

Rajan, B. (1965) 'The Indian Virtue'. *Journal of Commonwealth Literature* 1.

Rajan, Rajeswari Sunder (1986) 'After "Orientalism": Colonialism and English Literary Studies in India'. *Social Scientist* 158.

Rajan, Rajeswari Sunder (Ed.) (1992) *The Lie of the Land*. Delhi: Oxford University Press.

Rajan, Rajeswari Sunder (ed.) (1993) *Real and Imagined Women: Gender, Culture and Postcolonialism*. London: Routledge.

Ramachandra, Ragini (1991a) 'A Report on the Proceedings of a Four-day Seminar on Indian and Western Poetics at Work'. *The Literary Criterion* XXVI(2).

Ramachandra, Ragini (1991b) 'A Report of a Five-day Workshop on Commonwealth Literature'. *The Literary Criterion* XXVI(3).

Rao, Raja (1938) *Kanthapura*. Bombay: New Directions.

Rayan, Krishna (1984) 'The Case for an Indian Poetic Based on the Dhvani Theory'. *The Literary Criterion* XVII(2).

Raychaudhuri, Tapan (1988) *Perceptions of the West in Nineteenth Century Bengal*. Delhi: Oxford University Press.

Raza, Moonis (1990) *Education, Development and Society*. New Delhi: Vikas.

Redfield, Robert (1956) *Peasant, Society and Culture*. Chicago: Chicago University Press.

Robbins, Bruce (1993) *The Secular Vocation: Intellectuals, Professionalism, Culture*. London & New York: Verso.

Rostow, W.W. (1960) *The Stages of Economic Growth: A Non-Communist Manifesto*. London: Cambridge University Press.

Roy, Rammohun (1945-58) *The English Works of Rammohun Roy*. 6 parts. Eds. Kalidas Nag and Debajyoti Burman. Calcutta: Sadharan Brahmo Samaj.

Rushdie, Salman (1991) *Imaginary Homelands*. London: Granta.

Rushdie, Salman (1984) '"Errata": Unreliable Narration in Midnight's Children'. In *A Sense of Place: Essays in Post-Colonial Literatures*. Ed. Britta Olincter. Goteborg: Goteborg University Commonwealth Studies.

Said, Edward (1975) *Beginnings: Intention and Method*. New York: Columbia University Press.

Said, Edward (1979) *Orientalism*. New York: Vintage.

Said, Edward (1983) *The World, the Text, and the Critic*. London: Vintage.

Said, Edward (1986) 'Intellectuals in the Post-colonial World'. *Salmagundi* 70/71.

Said, Edward (1988) 'Identity, Negation and Violence'. *New Left Review* 171.

Said, Edward (1993) *Culture and Imperialism*. London: Chatto and Windus.

Sarkar, Jadunath (1973) *The History of Bengal. Muslim Period, 1200-1757*. Patna.

Sarkar, Sumit (1983) *Modern India 1885-1947*. London: Macmillan.

Sarkar, Sumit (1985) *A Critique of Colonial India*. Calcutta: Papyrus.

Sastry, L.S.R. Krishna (1993) 'Objectives and "Meaningfulness" of Research'. In *Provocations*. Eds. Sudhakar Marathe, Mohan Ramanan and Robert Bellarmine. Madras: Orient Longman in association with British Council.

Shahane, V.A. (ed.) (1975) *A Focus on* A Passage to India. Bombay: Orient Longman.

Sharpe, Jenny (1993) 'The Unspeakable Limits of Rape: Colonial Violence and Counter-Insurgency'. In *Colonial Discourse and Post-Colonial Theory*. Eds. Patrick Williams and Laura Chrisman. Hertfordshire: Harvester Wheatsleaf.

Shayer, David (1972) *The Teaching of English in Schools 1900-1970*. London: Routledge & Kegan Paul.

Sheth, D.L. (1990) 'No English Please, We're Indian'. In *The Illustrated Weekly of India*, August 19.

Sheth, D.L. (1992) 'Movements, Intellectuals and the State: Social Policy in Nation-Building'. *Economic and Political Weekly*, XXVII(8).

Sheth, D.L. (1995) 'The Great Language Debate: Politics of Metropolitan versus Vernacular India'. In *Crisis and Change in Modern India*. Eds. Upendra Baxi and Bhikhu Parekh. New Delhi: Sage.

Shils, Edward (1961) *The Intellectual between Tradition and Modernity: the Indian Situation*. The Hague: Mouton & Co.

Shiva, Vandana (1987) 'The Violence of a Reductionist Science'. *Alternatives* XII(2).

Shiva, Vandana (1988) *Staying Alive: Women, Ecology and Survival in India*. New Delhi: Kali for Women.

Shohat, Ella (1992) 'Notes on the "Post-Colonial"'. *Social Text* 31/32.

Shukla, P.D. (1983) *Administration of Education in India*. New Delhi: Vikas.

Shukla, P.D. (1987) *Towards the New Pattern of Education in India*. New Delhi: Sterling.

Sinfield, Alan (1993) 'The Politics of Englit Today'. Professorial Lecture at the University of Sussex.

Singh, Charu Sheel (1989) 'Figural Isotopes in Paul de Man's Literary Theory'. *The Literary Criterion* 23(4).

Singh, Frances B. (1985) 'A Passage to India, the National Movement, and Independence'. *Twentieth Century Literature* 31(2-3).

Sinha, D.P. (1964) *The Educational Policy of The East India Company in Bengal to 1854.* Calcutta: Punthi Pustak.

Sinha, S. and R. Bhattacharya (1969) '*Bhadralok* and *Chotolok* in a Rural Area of West Bengal'. *Sociological Bulletin* 18.

Smith, Anthony D. (1994) 'The Politics of Culture: Ethnicity and Nationalism'. In *Companion Encyclopedia of Anthropology.* Ed. T. Ingold. London: Routledge.

Smith, Barbara Herrnstein (1990) 'Cult-Lit: Hirsch, Literacy, and the "National Culture"'. *South Atlantic Quarterly* 89(1).

Spear, Percival (1963) *The Nabobs: A Study of Social Life of the English in the Eighteenth Century.* London: Oxford University Press.

Spivak, Gayatri Chakravorty (1985) 'Three Women's Texts and a Critique of Imperialism'. *Critical Inquiry* 12(1).

Spivak, Gayatri Chakravorty (1985a) 'The Rani Of Sirmur: An Essay in Reading the Archives'. *History and Theory* XXIV(3).

Spivak, Gayatri Chakravorty (1987) *In Other Worlds: Essays in Cultural Politics.* New York and London: Methuen.

Spivak, Gayatri Chakravorty (1987a) 'Speculations on Reading Marx: After Reading Derrida'. In *Poststructuralism and the Question of History.* Eds. Derek Atridge, Geoff Bennington and Robert Young. New York: Cambridge University Press.

Spivak, Gayatri Chakravorty (1988) 'Can the Subaltern Speak?' In *Marxism and the Interpretation of Culture.* Eds. Cary Nelson and Lawrence Grossberg. Urbana and Chicago: University of Illinois Press.

Spivak, Gayatri Chakravorty (1990) *The Post-Colonial Critic.* Ed. Sarah Harasym. London: Routledge.

Spivak, Gayatri Chakravorty (1990a) 'Poststructuralism, Marginality, Post-coloniality, and Value'. In *Literary Theory Today.* Eds. Peter Collier and Helga Geyer-Ryan. New York: Cornell University Press.

Spivak, Gayatri Chakravorty (1992) 'Woman in Difference: Maheswata Devi's "Douloti the Bountiful"'. In *Nationalism and Sexualities*. Eds. Andrew Parker et al. New York: Routledge.

Spivak, Gayatri Chakravorty (1993) 'The Burden of English'. In *Orientalism and the Postcolonial Predicament*. Eds. C. Breckenridge and P. van der Veer. Philadelphia: University of Pennsylvania Press.

Srivatsan, R. (1991) 'Photography and Society: Icon Building in Action'. *Economic and Political Weekly of India*, Annual Number, March.

Stallybrass, P. and Allon White (1986) *The Politics and Poetics of Transgression*. London: Methuen.

Stokes, Eric (1959) *The English Utilitarians and India*. Oxford: Clarendon Press.

Street, Brian V. (1975) *The Savage in Literature*. London: Routledge and Kegan Paul.

Street, Brian V. (1992) 'Literacy and Nationalism'. *History of European Ideas* 16(3).

Street, Brian V. (1993) 'Culture is a Verb: Anthropological Aspects of language as Cultural Process'. In *Language and Culture*. Eds. David Graddol, Linda Thompson and Mike Byram. Clevedon, Philadelphia, Adelaide: BAAL in association with Multilingual Matters Inc.

Street, Brian V. (1993a) *Cross-Cultural Approaches to Literacy*. Cambridge: Cambridge University Press.

Street, Brian V. (1994) 'Literacy and Power?'. *British Association for Literacy in Development* 10(1).

Suleri, Sara (1987) 'The Geography of *A Passage to India*'. In *Modern Critical Views: E.M. Forster*. Ed. Harold Bloom. New York, New Haven and Philadelphia: Chelsea House.

Suleri, Sara (1992) *The Rhetoric of English India*. Chicago: Chicago University Press.

Tagore, Rabindranath (1921) *Reminiscences*. London: Macmillan.

Tagore, Rabindranath (1961) *Towards Universal Man*. Bombay: Asia.

Thapar, Romila (1966) *A History of India.* Vol. 1. Harmondsworth: Penguin.

Thapar, Romila (1984) *From Lineage to State.* Bombay: Oxford University Press.

Thapar, Romila (1989) 'Imagined Religious Communities? Ancient History and the Modern Search for Hindu Identity'. *Modern Asian Studies* 23(2).

Tharu, S. and K. Lalitha (1991) *Women Writing in India.* Vol. 1. London: Pandora Press.

Thompson, Edward and G.T. Garrat (1958) *Rise and Fulfillment of British Rule In India.* Central Book Depot: Allahabad.

Thompson, John B. (1984) *Studies in the Theory of Ideology.* Polity Press: Cambridge.

The Times of India (1992) May 8.

Todorov, Tzvetan (1984) *Mikhail Bakhtin: the Dialogical Principle.* Minneapolis: University of Minnesota Press.

Trevelyan, C.E. (1838) *On the Education of the People of India.* London: Longman, Orme, Brown, Green and Longmans.

UNICEF (1991) *Basic Education and National Development: The Indian Scene.* New Delhi: UNICEF.

Upadhyay, Prakash Chandra (1992) 'The Politics of Indian Secularism'. *Modern Asian Studies* 26(4).

Varghese, N.V. and J.B.G. Tilak (1991) *The Financing of Education in India.* Paris: UNESCO.

Verma, Rajendra (1978) *Educational Planning and Poverty of India: A Comparative Study 1944-77.* New Delhi: Lancer.

Viswanathan, Gauri (1987) 'The Beginnings of English Literary Study in British India'. *Oxford Literary Review* 9.

Viswanathan, G. (1989) *The Masks Of Conquest: Literary Study and British Rule in India.* London: Faber & Faber.

Voloshinov, V.N. (1986) *Marxism and the Philosophy of Language.* Trans. L. Matejka and I.R. Titunik. Cambridge, Mass.: Harvard University Press.

Wallerstein, Immanuel (1974) 'The Rise and Future Demise of the World Capitalist System: Concepts for Comparative Analysis'. *Comparative Studies in Society and History* 16.

Walsh, Judith E. (1983) *Growing Up in British India: Indian Autobiographers on Childhood and Education under the Raj*. New York: Holmes and Meier.

Washbrook, David (1981) 'Law, State and Agrarian Society in Colonial India'. *Modern Asian Studies* 15(3).

Weiner, Myron (1991) *The Child and the State in India*. Princeton: Princeton University Press.

Widdowson, H.G. (1975) *Stylistics and the Teaching of Literature*. London: Longman.

Williams, Patrick (1993) '*Kim* and Orientalism'. In *Colonial Discourse and Post-Colonial Theory: A Reader*. Ed. and intro. by Patrick Williams and Laura Chrisman. Hertfordshire: Harvester Wheatsleaf.

Williams, Patrick and Laura Chrisman (eds.) (1993) *Colonial Discourse and Post-Colonial Theory: A Reader*. Hertfordshire: Harvester Wheatsleaf.

Williams, Raymond (1976) *Keywords: A Vocabulary of Culture and Society*. London: Fontana Press.

Williams, Raymond (1977) *Marxism and Literature*. London: Macmillan.

Williams, Raymond (1983) *Writing in Society*. London: Verso.

Williamson, Bill (1979) *Education, Social Structure and Development*. London: Macmillan.

Wolff, Janet (1993) 'The Global and the Specific: Reconciling Conflicting Theories of the Culture'. In *Culture, Globalization and the World System*. Ed. Anthony D. King. Binghamton: State University of New York.

Young, Robert (1990) *White Mythologies: Writing History and the West*. London and New York: Routledge.

Young, Robert (1991) 'Neocolonialism and the Secret Agent of Knowledge: Interview with Gayatri Chakravorty Spivak'. *Oxford Literary Review* 13.

Zurbuchen, Mary S. (1992) 'Wiping out English'. *Seminar* 391.

Index

education, vernacular
  129
Edwardes, Michael 67
Eliot, T.S. 101-2, 108,
  135, 145
elite 94, 128
elite, nationalist 125
elitist 102
Elphinstone,
  Mountstuart 69
Empress of India 17
Engels, Friedrich 86,
  126
English 60, 63-64,
  125-27, 153, 157
English, departments
  of (see depart-
  ments)
English, Indian 130
English, Indian
  literature in 137,
  144
English, Indian
  Literature in 32
English, Indian novel
  in 81
English, teaching 124,
  131
Englishness 120
Enlightenment, the
  19, 34, 39-40, 57,
  120, 126, 145
enunciation 31, 48,
  127, 163
Escobar, Arturo
  115-16, 163
essentialist 107
essentializing, strate-
  gic 34
ethnocentrism 99
Europe 11-12, 39,
  44-46

Evangelists, Clapham
  73
Ezekiel, Nissim 136

Fanon, Frantz 18, 46,
  50-52, 93-94
Farquhar, J.N. 85
Farrar, F.W. 89
Featherstone, Mike
  29
feminism 44, 134
feminist, first world
  37
field coverage 145-46
field, research 169
*Fifth Report from the
  Select Committee
  on the Affairs of
  the East India
  Company* 69
films, Bollywood 170
films, popular 172
First World 28, 34,
  43, 45
Fishman, J. 12
Forrest, G. 87
Forster, E.M. 9, 19,
  47, 124, 146-52
Foucault, Michel
  20-22, 61, 67, 99,
  115, 120-21, 170,
  172
France, Anatole 93
Francis, Philip 66
Frank, André Gunder
  49
Freitag, Sandra B. 118
fundamentalism, Hin-
  du 25, 172-73

Gadamer, H.G. 134
Gallie, W.B. 97
Gandhi, M.K. 18, 24,
  91-92, 148-49, 155,
  165
Garrat, G.T. 68
Garu, Lingam
  Lakshmaji Pantlu
  80, 93
Gates, Henry Louis, Jr.
  50-51
Gellner, Ernest 12,
  106
Ghosh, P.C. 56
Ghosh, Sankar 57
Gibb, H.A.R. 166
Gilchrist, John 68
Gilroy, Paul 120
Gladwin, Francis 68
globalisation 29
globalisation,
  resistance to 29
Gokak, V.K. 140-41,
  153
Goldberg, David Theo
  107
Gopal, Ram 31, 158
Gosse, Edmund 94
Graff, Gerald 132,
  145
Gramsci, Antonio 9,
  13, 33, 75, 166
Grant, Charles 63, 76,
  88, 99
Gray, John 97
Great Tradition 16
Guha, Ranajit 87
Gupta, Balmukunda
  14
Gupta, Kshetra 82
Gupta, S.C. Sen 56
Guptaji 156

system, educational
21, 78, 91
system, world
capitalist 49
systems, Hindu and
Muslim legal 65

Tagore, Rabindranath
83, 91, 112, 142, 144
Tarkachudamani,
Pandit Sasadhar 82
Tasso 82
Tattvabodhini Patrika
80
Taylor, Charles 119
teaching, English 160
technologies,
disciplinary 170
temporality 52
text 134-35, 139
text, the world as 41
texts, English literary
142
textuality 41
Thapar, Romila 15,
71, 104, 154
Tharu, S. 139, 141,
160
theories, post-
structuralist 32
theory (see also
Bhabha and Spivak)
134
theory, colonial
discourse 32
theory, development
117
theory, Dhvani 59

theory, literary and
cultural 131
theory, postcolonial
discourse 27
theory, poststructur-
alist 33
Third World 28,
34-36, 43, 45, 53-54,
115-16
Thompson, E.P. 120
Thompson, Edward
68
Thompson, John B. 20
Thornton, Robert 98
thought, nationalist
13, 82, 137, 148
time 15
time-lag 45
time scale 101
tradition 16, 22, 105,
119, 164, 171
tradition, Indian 119
tradition, liberal
discursive 151
tradition, liberal
humanist 101
tradition, state 15
traditions, Sanskrit 55
traditions, vernacular
139
transformation,
cultural 98
transgression 165
translation, Indian
literatures in 144
translations 105
Trevelyan, C.E. 70,
72, 80, 99, 139-40
truth, regimes of 64
Tulsidas 144

University Grants
Commission 167
University Grants
Commission Report
159
Upadhyay, Prakash C.
23
Upanishads 16
uprising of 1857 81
Utalitarians, the 73,
119

Vaishnava singers
160
Valmiki 144
value 41-43
value, theory of 42
Van der Veer, Peter 15
varna 66
Vedic instruction 79
Vellore 76
violence, communal
105
Virgil 82
Vishwa Hindu
Parishad 130
Viswanathan, G.
63-64, 69, 77, 90,
93, 99, 132, 160
Vivekananda, Swami
15-16, 82
Vloloshinov, V.N. 134
Vyasa 144

Wallerstein, Im-
manuel 28, 49
Walsh, Judith E. 81
Washbrook, David 62,
66